A BOOK OF MODERN PROSE

D1638181

HARRAP'S ENGLISH CLASSICS

COMUS AND SOME SHORTER POEMS OF MILTON
Edited by E. M. W. TILLYARD, Litt.D., F.B.A., formerly Master of Jesus College, Cambridge
and PHYLLIS B. TILLYARD, M.A., Girton College, Cambridge

MILTON: PARADISE LOST: BOOKS I AND II
Edited by E. M. W. TILLYARD, Litt.D., F.B.A., formerly Master of Jesus College, Cambridge
and PHYLLIS B. TILLYARD, M.A., Girton College, Cambridge

MILTON: PARADISE LOST: BOOKS IX AND X
Edited by E. M. W. TILLYARD, Litt.D., F.B.A., formerly Master of Jesus College, Cambridge

CHAUCER: THE PROLOGUE TO THE CANTERBURY TALES
Edited by R. T. DAVIES, M.A., Lecturer in English Literature, Liverpool University

CHAUCER: THE KNIGHT'S TALE
Edited by J. A. W. BENNETT, M.A., D.Phil., Professor of Mediæval and Renaissance English in
University of Cambridge

CHAUCER: THE PARDONER'S TALE
Edited by NEVILL COGHILL, M.A., F.R.S.L., formerly Merton Professor of English Literature in
University of Oxford, *and* CHRISTOPHER TOLKIEN, M.A., Fellow of New College, Oxford

CHAUCER: THE NUN'S PRIEST'S TALE
Edited by NEVILL COGHILL, M.A., F.R.S.L., formerly Merton Professor of English Literature in
University of Oxford, *and* CHRISTOPHER TOLKIEN, M.A., Fellow of New College, Oxford

CHAUCER: THE MAN OF LAW'S TALE
Edited by NEVILL COGHILL, M.A., F.R.S.L., formerly Merton Professor of English Literature in
University of Oxford, *and* CHRISTOPHER TOLKIEN, M.A., Fellow of New College, Oxford

TWENTIETH-CENTURY NARRATIVE POEMS
Compiled and edited by MAURICE WOLLMAN, M.A.

TEN TWENTIETH-CENTURY POETS
Edited by MAURICE WOLLMAN, M.A.

A BOOK OF MODERN PROSE
Edited by DOUGLAS BROWN, M.A., formerly of The Perse School, Cambridge

TWENTIETH-CENTURY SHORT STORIES
Edited by DOUGLAS R. BARNES, Senior English Master, Minchenden School, Southgate,
and R. F. EGFORD, Senior English Master, Selhurst Grammar School

TEN CONTEMPORARY POETS
Compiled and edited by MAURICE WOLLMAN, M.A.

STORIES IN MODERN VERSE
Compiled and edited by MAURICE WOLLMAN, M.A.

A BOOK OF
MODERN PROSE

SELECTED BY

DOUGLAS BROWN

formerly of The Perse School Cambridge

HARRAP   LONDON

First published in Great Britain 1957
by GEORGE G. HARRAP & CO. LTD
182 High Holborn, London WC1V 7AX

Reprinted: 1959; 1963; 1964; 1965; 1966; 1967; 1969;
1977; 1978 *(twice)*; 1979 *(twice)*

ISBN 0 245 53215 3

---

*Composed in Garamond type and printed by
Western Printing Services Ltd, Bristol*

Made in Great Britain

Acknowledgments

I WISH to thank the authors and publishers whose names appear below for giving permission to reprint copyright material:

Mrs Frieda Lawrence and Messrs William Heinemann, Ltd, for "Nottingham and the Mining Country" and for an excerpt from "Flowery Tuscany," both first published in *Phoenix*; the author and The Hogarth Press, Ltd, for an excerpt from *An Autobiography*, by Edwin Muir; the author and Messrs A. D. Peters, for a chapter from *Undertones of War*, by Edmund Blunden; the author and Messrs Faber and Faber, Ltd, for an excerpt from *The Complete Memoirs of George Sherston*, by Siegfried Sassoon; the author and Messrs Jonathan Cape, Ltd, for two excerpts from *Good-bye to All That*, by Robert Graves; Messrs Jonathan Cape, Ltd, for an excerpt from *Autobiography*, by Eric Gill; Messrs Longmans, Green and Co., Ltd, for a series of extracts from a chapter of *My Apprenticeship*, by Beatrice Webb; the author and Messrs Edward Arnold, Ltd, for an excerpt from *Goldsworthy Lowes Dickinson*, by E. M. Forster; the Syndics of the Cambridge University Press for an excerpt from *Man on his Nature*, by Sir Charles Sherrington, and for two excerpts from *The Wheelwright's Shop*, by George Sturt; Messrs J. M.

Dent and Sons, Ltd, for an excerpt from *The Mirror of the Sea*, by Joseph Conrad, and for two excerpts from *The South Country*, by Edward Thomas; Mr Leonard Woolf for the essay "Joseph Conrad," from *The Common Reader*, by Virginia Woolf; and Messrs G. Bell and Sons, Ltd, for two excerpts from *Concerning the Nature of Things*, by Sir William Bragg.

    I wish to thank, too, many friends and colleagues whose suggestions and advice have helped me to choose and arrange these readings. In particular I am indebted to Mr G. H. Bantock, of the University College of Leicester. Nor would it be right, having regard to the purpose and scope of a book like this, to leave unacknowledged the prompting and directing of my reading and interests over many years by the nineteen volumes of the journal *Scrutiny*, published from 1932 to 1955.

D.B.

Contents

Introduction

I HAVE chosen substantial passages from the work of fourteen authors to suggest the range and the distinction of modern English prose. Each passage compares closely with at least one other; more subtle cross-currents run to and fro over the whole collection. The readings are so arranged as to make an image of our time. They indicate some of the deeper forces that have shaped our inheritance and affect us still. The first two take account of the changed environment of twentieth-century life, of psychology and of the deeper self-consciousness of modern men and women. The next sequence shows how the terrible experiences of trench warfare in the First World War disturbed and disordered men, and shattered earlier securities of belief and outlook. Four readings take us behind the scenes of movements like those associated with the Fabian Socialists and with Bloomsbury, offer protest against some trends in modern civilization, and make claims for the value of traditional wisdom, of religious faith, of personal relations, of the ways and crafts of the countryside. The last six relate different aspects of the artist's and the scientist's ways of regarding the world about us, and our experience of it.

For the understanding and enjoyment of these readings you will need a good dictionary but not an apparatus of notes. A very little research will elucidate, I
think, any reference not touched upon in the short
commentaries. Other problems will become clearer if
you look into the book from which the excerpt comes.
But there are difficulties here, not of the sort that notes
would help with. They are here because these writers
deal with important or subtle or profound issues. These
difficulties we have to face and grapple with as best
we may. We are not called upon to agree with everything the writers say. Rather, we are challenged by their
clear and vigorous feeling and thinking, and we have to
try to feel and to think more adequately ourselves. Perhaps I ought to add a special note about the three passages on experiences of the First World War. Those
who are sensitive, and quick to feel, may find them too
distressing. They, and others, may think these occupy
too large a space in the collection. But I believe this
entry into a world of horror and degradation really
was a turning-point for our age, an end and a beginning.
We cannot properly understand ourselves, our situation, or our literature unless we take full account of it.

Obviously this is not a lightweight volume. It contains the work of men and women of fine stamina and
resource, and the reader has to meet them on their
ground. I have set aside the writing often classified as
Belles-lettres or presented as *Essays*. I have set aside
writing for the sake of writing, all exhibition of 'style'
and the purple passage. I suppose these mannered
forms, with their disengaged and superficial interest
in what appears to be their subject matter, have some

value; but it is a small value. It has little to do with
the literature of prose. It cannot really help anyone
who wants to write well himself: that is, someone who
has something to say worth saying well. Instead I have
looked for three virtues: transparency of style, seriousness of purpose, and distinction of personality. So it
may be no accident that five of these authors are poets
in their own right, four others novelists, four others
men or women of notable achievement in one professional sphere or another.

As to transparency, I think of the virtue D. H.
Lawrence, and T. S. Eliot quoting him, have spoken
for in modern poetry; it is also a virtue of the finest
prose. "*. . . In this age of stark and unlovely actualities, a
stark directness, without a shadow of a lie, or a shadow of
deflexion anywhere. Everything can go but this stark, bare,
rocky directness of statement. . . .*" This attestation of the
man E. M. Forster called the greatest imaginative
novelist of our generation, comes from a letter of 1916;
it may serve as a pointer. It is so that we come to see
and to feel (and here I take the phrases from our
greatest living poet) *not the writing itself, but what we are
to see and to feel through the writing.* That is what the best
moments, at least, in these readings, have to offer us.

I

The Human Spirit
and the Modern World

D. H. Lawrence   :   *Phoenix*

Edwin Muir   :   *An Autobiography*

Nottingham and the Mining Country
D. H. Lawrence

'Nottingham and the Mining Country' begins with Lawrence himself, but in next to no time it becomes a penetrating report and a verdict upon the environment in which he grew up. His father was a miner who had worked at Brinsley Colliery from boyhood. Lawrence became an Elementary School teacher; but he began his first novel while attending Nottingham University, and soon he abandoned teaching for writing. His importance resides chiefly in a series of novels and a collection of short stories, original, imaginative, and disturbing. He travelled very widely during the 1920's, in a long endeavour to come to terms with himself and the world he lived in; but he composed this piece at the end of those travels, when he returned to England for a brief while in 1929. In September of the same year he became seriously ill, and he died in the spring of 1930 at Vence in the south of France.

Here is writing that touches on one after another of the deeper and more urgent aspects of the twentieth-century environment. The prose may seem at first to be informal to the point of carelessness. But gradually, as you take the feel of it, you may find the apparent carelessness to be a way of conveying very exactly a tone of voice, a quality of emphasis or conviction or irony, a delicate balance of temperate suggestion and deliberate exaggeration. You may wonder if this easy mastery of tone could be gained in any other way.

I was born nearly forty-four years ago, in Eastwood, a mining village of some three thousand souls, about eight miles from Nottingham, and one mile from the small stream, the Erewash, which divides Nottinghamshire from Derbyshire. It is hilly country, looking west to Crich and towards Matlock, sixteen miles away, and east and north-east towards Mansfield and the Sherwood Forest district. To me it seemed and still seems an extremely beautiful countryside, just between the red sandstone and the oak-trees of Nottingham, and the cold limestone, the ash-trees, the stone fences of Derbyshire. To me, as a child and a young man, it was still the old England of the forest and agricultural past; there were no motor-cars, the mines were, in a sense, an accident in the landscape, and Robin Hood and his merry men were not very far away.

The string of coal-mines of B. W. & Co. had been opened some sixty years before I was born, and Eastwood had come into being as a consequence. It must have been a tiny village at the beginning of the nineteenth century, a small place of cottages and fragmentary rows of little four-roomed miners' dwellings, the homes of the old colliers of the eighteenth century, who worked in the bits of mines, foot-hill mines with an opening in the hillside into which the miners walked, or windlass mines, where the men were wound up one at a time, in a bucket, by a donkey. The windlass mines were still working when my father was a boy—and the shafts of some were still there, when I was a boy.

But somewhere about 1820 the company must have sunk the first big shaft—not very deep—and installed the first machinery of the real industrial colliery. Then came my grandfather, a young man trained to be a tailor, drifting from the south of England, and got the job of company tailor for the Brinsley mine. In those days the company supplied the men with the thick flannel vests, or singlets, and the moleskin trousers lined at the top with flannel, in which the colliers worked. I remember the great rolls of coarse flannel and pit-cloth which stood in the corner of my grandfather's shop when I was a small boy, and the big, strange old sewing-machine, like nothing else on earth, which sewed the massive pit-trousers. But when I was only a child the company discontinued supplying the men with pit-clothes.

My grandfather settled in an old cottage down in a quarry-bed, by the brook at Old Brinsley, near the pit. A mile away, up at Eastwood, the company built the first miners' dwellings—it must be nearly a hundred years ago. Now Eastwood occupies a lovely position on a hilltop, with the steep slope towards Derbyshire and the long slope towards Nottingham. They put up a new church, which stands fine and commanding, even if it has no real form, looking across the awful Erewash Valley at the church of Heanor, similarly commanding, away on a hill beyond. What opportunities, what opportunities! These mining villages *might* have been like the lovely hill-towns of Italy, shapely and fascinating. And what happened?

Most of the little rows of dwellings of the old-style miners were pulled down, and dull little shops began to rise along the Nottingham Road, while on the down-slope of the north-side the company erected what is still known as the New Buildings, or the Square. These New Buildings consist of two great hollow squares of dwellings planked down on the rough slope of the hill, little four-room houses with the 'front' looking out-ward into the grim, blank street, and the 'back,' with a tiny square brick yard, a low wall, and a w.c. and ash-pit, looking into the desert of the square, hard, uneven, jolting black earth tilting rather steeply down, with these little back yards all round, and openings at the corners. The squares were quite big, and absolutely desert, save for the posts for clothes lines, and people passing, children playing on the hard earth. And they were shut in like a barracks enclosure, very strange.

Even fifty years ago the squares were unpopular. It was 'common' to live in the Square. It was a little less common to live in the Breach, which consisted of six blocks of rather more pretentious dwellings erected by the company in the valley below, two rows of three blocks, with an alley between. And it was most 'common,' most degraded of all to live in Dakins Row, two rows of the old dwellings, very old, black four-roomed little places, that stood on the hill again, not far from the Square.

So the place started. Down the steep street between the squares, Scargill Street, the Wesleyans' chapel was put up, and I was born in the little corner shop just above. Across the other side of the Square the miners themselves built the big, barn-like Primitive Methodist chapel. Along the hill-top ran the Nottingham Road, with its scrappy, ugly mid-Victorian shops. The little market-place, with a superb outlook, ended the village on the Derbyshire side, and was just here left bare, with the Sun Inn on one side, the chemist across, with the gilt pestle-and-mortar, and a shop at the other corner, the corner of Alfreton Road and Nottingham Road.

In this queer jumble of the old England and the new, I came into consciousness. As I remember, little local speculators already began to straggle dwellings in rows, always in rows, across the fields; nasty red-brick, flat-faced dwellings with dark slate roofs. The bay-window period only began when I was a child. But most of the country was untouched.

There must be three or four hundred company houses in the squares and the streets that surround the squares, like a great barracks wall. There must be sixty or eighty company houses in the Breach. The old Dakins Row will have thirty to forty little holes. Then counting the old cottages and rows left with their old gardens down the lanes and along the twitchells, and even in the midst of Nottingham Road itself, there were houses enough for the population, there was no need for much building. And not much building went on when I was small.

We lived in the Breach, in a corner house. A field-path came down under a great hawthorn hedge. On the other side was the brook, with the old sheep-bridge going over into the meadows. The hawthorn hedge by the brook had grown tall as tall trees, and we used to bathe from there in the dipping-hole, where the sheep were dipped, just near the fall from the old mill-dam, where the water rushed. The mill only ceased grinding the local corn when I was a child. And my father, who always worked in Brinsley pit, and who always got up at five o'clock, if not at four, would set off in the dawn across the fields at Coney Grey, and hunt for mushrooms in the long grass, or perhaps pick up a skulking rabbit, which he would bring home at evening inside the lining of his pit-coat.

So that the life was a curious cross between industrialism and the old agricultural England of Shakespeare and Milton and Fielding and George Eliot. The dialect was broad Derbyshire, and always 'thee' and 'thou.' The people lived almost entirely by instinct, men of my father's age could not really read. And the pit did not mechanize men. On the contrary. Under the butty system, the miners worked underground as a sort of intimate community, they knew each other practically naked, and with curious close intimacy, and the darkness and the underground remoteness of the pit 'stall,' and the continual presence of danger, made the physical, instinctive, and intuitional contact between men very highly developed, a contact almost as close as touch, very real and very powerful. This physical awareness and intimate *togetherness* was at its strongest down pit. When the men came up into the light, they blinked. They had, in a measure, to change their flow. Nevertheless, they brought with them above ground the curious dark intimacy of the mine, the naked sort of contact, and if I think of my childhood, it is always as if there was a lustrous sort of inner darkness, like the gloss of coal, in which we moved and had our real being. My father loved the pit. He was hurt badly, more than once, but he would never stay away. He loved the contact, the intimacy, as men in the war loved the intense male comradeship of the dark days. They did not know what they had lost till they lost it. And I think it is the same with the young colliers of today.

Now the colliers had also an instinct of beauty. The colliers' wives had not. The colliers were deeply alive, instinctively. But they had no daytime ambition, and no daytime intellect. They avoided, really, the rational aspect of life. They preferred to take life instinctively and intuitively. They didn't even care very profoundly about wages. It was the women, naturally, who nagged on this score. There was a big discrepancy, when I was a boy, between the collier who saw, at the best, only a brief few hours of daylight—often no daylight at all during the winter weeks—and the collier's wife, who had all the day to herself when the man was down pit.

The great fallacy is, to pity the man. He didn't dream of pitying himself, till agitators and sentimentalists taught him to. He was happy: or more than happy, he was fulfilled. Or he was fulfilled on the receptive side, not on the expressive. The collier went to the pub and drank in order to continue his intimacy with his mates. They talked endlessly, but it was rather of wonders and marvels, even in politics, than of facts. It was hard facts, in the shape of wife, money, and nagging home necessities, which they fled away from, out of the house to the pub, and out of the house to the pit.

The collier fled out of the house as soon as he could, away from the nagging materialism of the woman. With the women it was always: This is broken, now you've got to mend it! or else: We want this, that and the other, and where is the money coming from? The collier didn't know and didn't care very deeply—his life was otherwise. So he escaped. He roved the countryside with his dog, prowling for a rabbit, for nests, for mushrooms, anything. He loved the countryside, just the indiscriminating feel of it. Or he loved just to sit on his heels and watch—anything or nothing. He was not intellectually interested. Life for him did not consist in facts, but in a flow. Very often he loved his garden. And very often he had a genuine love of the beauty of flowers. I have known it often and often, in colliers.

Now the love of flowers is a very misleading thing. Most women love flowers as possessions, and as trimmings. They can't look at a flower, and wonder a moment, and pass on. If they see a flower that arrests their attention, they must at once pick it, pluck it. Possession! A possession! Something added on *to me*! And most of the so-called love of flowers today is merely this reaching out of possession and egoism: something I've *got*: something that embellishes *me*. Yet I've seen many a collier stand in his back garden looking down at a flower with that odd, remote sort of contemplation which shows a *real* awareness of the presence of beauty. It would not even be admiration, or joy, or delight, or any of those things which so often have a root in the possessive instinct. It would be a sort of contemplation: which shows the incipient artist.

The real tragedy of England, as I see it, is the tragedy of ugliness. The country is so lovely: the man-made England is so vile. I know that the ordinary collier, when I was a boy, had a peculiar sense of beauty, coming from his intuitive and instinctive consciousness, which was awakened down pit. And the fact that he met with just cold ugliness and raw materialism when he came up into daylight, and particularly when he came to the Square or the Breach, and to his own table, killed something in him, and in a sense spoiled him as a man. The woman almost invariably nagged about material things. She was taught to do it; she was encouraged to do it. It was a mother's business to see that her sons 'got on,' and it was the man's business to provide the money. In my father's generation, with the old wild England behind them, and the lack of education, the man was not beaten down. But in my generation, the boys I went to school with, colliers now, have all been beaten down, what with the din-din-dinning of Board Schools, books, cinemas, clergymen, the whole national and human consciousness hammering on the fact of material prosperity above all things.

The men are beaten down, there is prosperity for a time, in their defeat—and then disaster looms ahead. The root of all disaster is disheartenment. And men are disheartened. The men of England, the colliers in particular, are disheartened. They have been betrayed and beaten.

Now though perhaps nobody knew it, it was ugliness which betrayed the spirit of man, in the nineteenth century. The great crime which the moneyed classes and promoters of industry committed in the Palmy Victorian days was the condemning of the workers to ugliness, ugliness, ugliness; meanness and formless and ugly surroundings, ugly ideals, ugly religion, ugly hope, ugly love, ugly clothes, ugly furniture, ugly houses, ugly relationship between workers and employers. The human soul needs actual beauty even more than bread. The middle classes jeer at the colliers for buying pianos—but what is the piano, often as not, but a blind reaching out for beauty? To the woman it is a possession and a piece of furniture and something to feel superior about. But see the elderly colliers trying to learn to play, see them listening with queer alert faces to their daughter's execution of *The Maiden's Prayer*, and you will see a blind, unsatisfied craving for beauty. It is far more deep in the men than in the women. The women want show. The men want beauty, and still want it.

If the company, instead of building those sordid and hideous Squares, then, when they had that lovely site to play with, there on the hill top; if they had put a tall column in the middle of the small market-place, and run three parts of a circle of arcade round the pleasant space, where people could stroll or sit, and with the handsome houses behind! If they had made big substantial houses, in apartments of five and six rooms, and with handsome entrances. If above all, they had encouraged song and dancing—for the miners still sang and danced—and provided handsome space for these. If only they had encouraged some form of beauty in dress, some form of beauty in interior life—furniture, decoration. If they had given prizes for the handsomest chair or table, the loveliest scarf, the most charming room that the men or women could make! If only they had done this, there would never have been an industrial problem. The industrial problem arises from the base forcing of all human energy into a competition of mere acquisition.

You may say the working man would not have accepted such a form of life; the Englishman's home is his castle, etc., etc.—'my own little home.' But if you can hear every word the next-door-people say, there's not much castle. And if you can see everybody in the square if they go to the w.c.! And if your one desire is to get out of the 'castle' and your 'own little home'!— well, there's not much to be said for it. Anyhow it's only the woman who idolizes 'her own little home'— and it's always the woman at her worst, her most greedy, most possessive, most mean. There's nothing to be said for the 'little home' any more: a great scrabble of ugly pettiness over the face of the land.

As a matter of fact, till 1800 the English people were strictly a rural people—very rural. England has had towns for centuries, but they have never been real towns, only clusters of village streets. Never the real *urbs*. The English character has failed to develop the real *urban* side of a man, the civic side. Siena is a bit of a place, but it is a real city, with citizens intimately connected with the city. Nottingham is a vast place sprawling towards a million, and it is nothing more than an amorphous agglomeration. There *is* no Nottingham, in the sense that there is Siena. The Englishman is stupidly undeveloped, as a citizen. And it is partly due to his 'little home' stunt, and partly to his acceptance of hopeless paltriness in his surrounding. The new cities of America are much more genuine cities, in the Roman sense, than is London or Manchester. Even Edinburgh used to be more of a true city than any town England ever produced.

That silly little individualism of 'the Englishman's home is his castle' and 'my own little home' is out of date. It would work almost up to 1800, when every Englishman was still a villager, and a cottager. But the industrial system has brought a great change. The Englishman still likes to think of himself as a 'cottager'—'my home, my garden.' But it is puerile. Even the farm labourer today is psychologically a town-bird. The English are town-birds through and through, today, as the inevitable result of their complete industrialization. Yet they don't know how to build a city, how to think of one, or how to live in one. They are all suburban, pseudo-cottagy, and not one of them knows how to be truly urban—the citizens as the Romans were citizens—or the Athenians—or even the Parisians, till the war came.

And this is because we have frustrated that instinct of community which would make us unite in pride and dignity in the bigger gesture of the citizen, not the cottager. The great city means beauty, dignity, and a certain splendour. This is the side of the Englishman that has been thwarted and shockingly betrayed. England is a mean and petty scrabble of paltry dwellings called 'homes.' I believe in their heart of hearts all Englishmen loathe their little homes—but not the women. What we want is a bigger gesture, a greater scope, a certain splendour, a certain grandeur, and beauty, big beauty. The American does far better than we, in this.

And the promoter of industry, a hundred years ago,

dared to perpetrate the ugliness of my native village. And still more monstrous, promoters of industry today are scrabbling over the face of England with miles and square miles of red-brick 'homes,' like horrible scabs. And the men inside these little red rat-traps get more and more helpless, being more and more humiliated, more and more dissatisfied, like trapped rats. Only the meaner sort of women go on loving the little home which is no more than a rat-trap to her man.

Do away with it all, then. At no matter what cost, start in to alter it. Never mind about wages and industrial squabbling. Turn the attention elsewhere. Pull down my native village to the last brick. Plan a nucleus. Fix the focus. Make a handsome gesture of radiation from the focus. And then put up big buildings, handsome, that sweep to a civic centre. And furnish them with beauty. And make an absolute clean start. Do it place by place. Make a new England. Away with little homes! Away with scrabbling pettiness and paltriness. Look at the contours of the land, and build up from these, with a sufficient nobility. The English may be mentally or spiritually developed. But as citizens of splendid cities they are more ignominious than rabbits. And they nag, nag, nag all the time about politics and wages and all that, like mean narrow housewives.

From " Phoenix "

Few will want to go all the way with every sentence of that; fewer still will be unaffected and unchallenged by it. Twenty-five years have passed, but the sharpest of these insights still hold, for Lawrence pushes down to the roots. The opening chapters of his novel "Sons and Lovers" (in which he makes imaginative use of Eastwood, and his own and his family's experiences there) compare very interestingly with this piece; and the vigorous paragraphs here about possessiveness and contemplation sound a note to be heard again in later readings.

There are short stories that deal with the mining community among Lawrence's "Tales" and many more that take up the kind of issue this piece has raised. His most thorough and wide-ranging picture of this growth of our life out of earlier ways is to be found in the novel "The Rainbow." 'Nottingham and the Mining Country' is published in a Penguin "Selected Essays," and Penguin Books have published most of his best novels and stories.

A Boy's Dreams
Edwin Muir

*This passage from Edwin Muir's "An Autobiography"
concludes another account of an environment. This time the
environment is the seemingly remote life of Orkney at the
end of the last century, a life whose roots were deeply sunk
in the abiding past. Dr Muir's description of it gives a
vivid feeling of some of the humanly important things that
seem to have been lost to-day. Now he turns his reflections
to the private and personal world of the boy who was born
in Orkney in 1887.*

*Dr Muir moved with his family to Glasgow when he was
fourteen. He left school, and worked in a variety of places,
severely handicapped by ill health. In the 1920's while
Lawrence and his wife were exploring Australia, Ceylon,
Mexico, Dr Muir and Willa, his wife, were exploring
Europe. Together they undertook the translation of the
novels of Kafka ("The Trial" is available as a Penguin),
and Dr Muir achieved distinction as a critic and a poet.
During the Second World War he lived and worked in
Scotland, but afterwards he returned to Prague for a while,
and to Rome, as an officer of the British Council. Later
he was Warden of Newbattle Abbey College near Edinburgh,
a residential college for adult education.*

He died in Cambridge in 1959.

I HAVE always been fascinated by a part of us about
which we know far less than our remote ancestors
did: the part which divined those immediate though

concealed relations that made them endow their heroes with the qualities of the animals whose virtues they incarnated, calling a man a bull for strength, a lion for courage, or a fox for cunning. That age is fabulous to us, populated by heraldic men and legendary beasts. We see a reflection of it in the Indian reliefs where saints and crowned emperors wander among tigers, elephants, and monkeys, and in the winged bulls of the Assyrians with their human heads: angel, beast, and man in one. The age which felt this connection between men and animals was so much longer than the brief historical period known to us that we cannot conceive it; but our unconscious life goes back into it. In that age everything was legendary, and the creatures went about like characters in a parable of beasts. Some of them were sacred and some monstrous, some quaint and ugly as house gods; they were worshipped and sacrificed; they were hunted; and the hunt, like the worship and the sacrifice, was a ritual act. They were protagonists in the first sylvan war, half human and half pelted and feathered, from which rose the hearth, the community, and the arts. Man felt guilty towards them, for he took their lives day after day, in obedience to a custom so long established that no one could say when it began. Though he killed them, they were sacred to him, because without destroying them he could not live; and so when they lay in heaps, in hecatombs, they were a vast sacrifice offered by the animal kingdom, and they gave their lives in hundreds of thousands, guiltlessly, by a decree of destiny. Man tamed some of them and yoked them to the plough and the mill; he fattened them so that he might eat

their flesh; he drank their milk, used their fleeces and
their hides to clothe him, their horns as ornaments or
goblets, and lived with them under the same roof. This
went on for ages beside which the age we know is
hardly more than a day. As their life had to be taken
and the guilt for it accepted, the way of taking it was
important, and the ritual arose, in which were united
the ideas of necessity and guilt, turning the killing into
a mystery.

My passion for animals comes partly from being
brought up so close to them, in a place where people
lived as they had lived for two hundred years; partly
from I do not know where. Two hundred years ago
the majority of people lived close to the animals by
whose labour or flesh they existed. The fact that we
live on these animals remains; but the personal relation is gone, and with it the very ideas of necessity
and guilt. The animals we eat are killed by thousands
in slaughter-houses which we never see. A rationalist
would smile at the thought that there is any guilt at
all: there is only the necessity, he would say, a necessity
which is laid upon all carnivores, not on man only.
But our dreams and ancestral memories speak a
different language. As it is, the vegetarians are more
honest than the rest of us, though their alternative is
probably a false one, for they merely avoid the guilt
instead of accepting it.

I do not know whether many people have dreams of
animals; perhaps these dreams die out in families which
have lived for two or three generations in a big city;
I have no means of knowing. But it is certain that
people who have been brought up in close contact

with animals, including the vast majority of the generations from whom we spring, have dreamed, and dream
of animals, and my own experience shows that these
dreams are often tinged with a guilt of which consciously we are unaware. As I feel that these dreams go
back to my world as a child, the best place to speak of
them is here. If I were recreating my life in an autobiographical novel I could bring out these correspon-
dences freely and show how our first intuition of the
world expands into vaster and vaster images, creating a
myth which we act almost without knowing it, while
our outward life goes on its ordinary routine of eating,
drinking, sleeping, working, and making money in
order to beget sons and daughters who will do the
same. I could follow these images freely if I were
writing an autobiographical novel. As it is, I have to
stick to the facts and try to fit them in where they will
fit in.

It is clear that no autobiography can begin with a
man's birth, that we extend far beyond any boundary
line which we can set for ourselves in the past or the
future, and that the life of every man is an endlessly
repeated performance of the life of man. It is clear for
the same reason that no autobiography can confine
itself to conscious life, and that sleep, in which we pass
a third of our existence, is a mode of experience, and
our dreams a part of reality. In themselves our conscious lives may not be particularly interesting. But
what we are not and can never be, our fable, seems to
me inconceivably interesting. I should like to write

that fable, but I cannot even live it; and all I could do if I related the outward course of my life would be to show how I have deviated from it; though even that is impossible, since I do not know the fable or anybody who knows it. One or two stages in it I can recognize: the age of innocence and the Fall and all the dramatic consequences which issue from the Fall. But these lie behind experience, not on its surface; they are not historical events; they are stages in the fable.

The problem that confronts an autobiographer even more urgently than other men is, How can he know himself? I am writing about myself in this book, yet I do not know what I am. I know my name, the date and place of my birth, the appearance of the places I have lived in, the people I have met, the things I have done. I know something of the society which dictates many of my actions, thoughts, and feelings. I know a little about history, and can explain to myself in a rough-and-ready fashion how that society came into being. But I know all this in an external and deceptive way, as if it were a dry legend which I had made up in collusion with mankind. This legend is founded on a sort of agreement such as children presuppose in their games of make-believe: an agreement by which years and days are given certain numbers to distinguish them, and peoples and countries and other things certain names: all this is necessary, of course, for the business of living. But it is a deception as well: if I knew all these figures and names I should still not know myself, far less all the other people in the world, or the small number whom I call friends. This external approach, no matter how perfect, will never teach me much either about them or about myself.

Take the appearance of a man, which is supposed to tell so much about him. He can never see that appearance: he can never see himself. If he looks at his face in a mirror, which faithfully reflects not only him, but the anxiety or hope with which he stares into it, he does not feel that this is himself. The face he sees has a certain convincing quality, it is true, like all faces; there is experience, thought, evasion, resolution, success, failure, suffering, and a certain comfort in it; there is in it everything that one can ask from a face. It imposes without effort—there can be no doubt of that—on every one else. He knows that it was made by him and time in a curious, often reluctant collaboration, and time is so much the stronger partner that at certain moments there seems to be nothing there but time. For though he incised every line himself—with no idea that these lines would remain—time fixed each of them by a principle of selection which had no regard whatever for him. If he looks honestly at the result it is time that convinces him, time that tells him, "You must accept this, for I have preserved it." Yet what time preserves is not what he would have liked to preserve. So that there are moments when he is so oppressed by this face which he carries about wherever he goes that he would like to take it down and put it up again differently; but only death can do that. There is no getting away from this result of time's collaboration. This face constructed to look like a face has an absolute plausibility. Yet if the man sees that face in a photograph it looks like the face of a stranger.

Or take a man's action. We may know that he works in an office or in a coal-mine, that he has made a great deal of money by speculating on the Stock Exchange, that he once reached the South Pole, that he governed a province in India, that he won a race, that he threw up his post to nurse lepers or save the souls of heathens. These things tell us something about him; working in an office, winning money on the Stock Exchange, reaching the South Pole, and converting heathens leave their mark on a man, and *condition* him. A clerk is not like a coal-miner, or a stockbroker like an explorer. It is the same with countless other things. A man who lives in Kensington is different from a man who lives in Wapping. The differences are important, and they are caused by various distortions. It distorts a man to work in a coal-mine or an office; it distorts him in a different way to make a fortune on the Stock Exchange, though in a commercial society the distortion may be less apparent. It need not distort a man so much to be an explorer or a missionary. The miner cannot live a civilized life, and society sins against him; the stockbroker will not live a civilized life, and sins against society. Or at any rate the sin is there, though it is difficult to establish where its roots lie. These things are of enormous importance, and we shall never settle them until the miner and the stockbroker live a civilized life.

But they are not of much help to us when we set out to discover what we are, and there is a necessity in us, however blind and ineffectual, to discover what we are. Religion once supplied that knowledge, but our life is no longer ruled by religion. Yet we can know

what we are only if we accept some of the hypotheses
of religion. Human beings are understandable only as
immortal spirits; they become natural then, as natural
as young horses; they are absolutely unnatural if we
try to think of them as a mere part of the natural world.
They are immortal spirits distorted and corrupted in
countless ways by the world into which they are born;
bearing countless shapes, beautiful, quaint, grotesque;
living countless lives, trivial, sensational, dull; serving
behind counters, going to greyhound races, playing
billiards, preaching to savages in Africa, collecting
stamps, stalking deer in the Highlands, adding up
figures in an office for fifty years, ruining one another
in business, inventing explosives which will destroy
other men and women on a large scale, praying for
the cessation of war, weeping over their sins, or trying
to discover what sin really is: doing everything that is
conceivable for human beings to do, and doing it in a
different way at every stage of history. I do not have
the power to prove that man is immortal and that the
soul exists; but I know that there must be such a proof,
and that compared with it every other demonstration
is idle. It is true that human life without immortality
would be inconceivable to me, though that is not the
ground for my belief. It would be inconceivable because if man is an animal by direct descent I can see
human life only as a nightmare populated by animals
wearing top hats and kid gloves, painting their lips and
touching up their cheeks and talking in heated rooms,
rubbing their muzzles together in the moment of lust,
going through innumerable clever tricks, learning
to make and listen to music, to gaze sentimentally at

sunsets, to count, to acquire a sense of humour, to give their lives for some cause, or to pray.

This picture has always been in my mind since one summer evening in Glasgow in 1919. I did not believe in the immortality of the soul at that time; I was deep in the study of Nietzsche, and had cast off with a great sense of liberation all belief in any other life than the life we live here and now, as an imputation on the purity of immediate experience, which I had intellectually convinced myself was guiltless and beyond good and evil. I was returning in a tramcar from my work; the tramcar was full and very hot; the sun burned through the glass on backs of necks, shoulders, faces, trousers, skirts, hands, all stacked there impartially. Opposite me was sitting a man with a face like a pig's, and as I looked at him in the oppressive heat the words came into my mind, "That is an animal." I looked round me at the other people in the tramcar; I was conscious that something had fallen from them and from me; and with a sense of desolation I saw that they were all animals, some of them good, some evil, some charming, some sad, some happy, some sick, some well. The tramcar stopped and went on again, carrying its menagerie; my mind saw countless other tramcars where animals sat or got on or off with mechanical dexterity, as if they had been trained in a circus; and I realized that in all Glasgow, in all Scotland, in all the world, there was nothing but millions of such creatures living an animal life and moving towards an animal death as towards a great slaughter-house. I stared at the faces, trying to make them human again and to dispel the hallucination, but I could not.

This experience was so terrifying that I dismissed it, deliberately forgot it by that perverse power which the mind has of obliterating itself. I felt as if I had lived for a few moments in Swift's world, for Swift's vision of humanity was the animal vision. I could not have endured it for more than a few minutes. I did not associate it at the time with Nietzsche. But I realized that I could not bear mankind as a swarming race of thinking animals, and that if there was not somewhere, it did not matter where—in a suburb of Glasgow or of Hong Kong or of Honolulu—a single living soul, life was a curious, irrelevant desolation. I pushed away this realization for a time, but it returned again later, like the memory of my cowardice as a boy.

The animal world is a great impersonal order, without pathos in its suffering. Man is bound to it by necessity and guilt, and by the closer bond of life, for he breathes the same breath. But when man is swallowed up in nature nature is corrupted and man is corrupted. The sense of corruption in *King Lear* comes from the fact that Goneril, Regan, and Cornwall are merely animals furnished with human faculties as with weapons which they can take up or lay down at will, faculties which they have stolen, not inherited. Words are their teeth and claws, and thought the technique of the deadly spring. They are so *unnatural* in belonging completely to nature that Gloucester can explain them only by "these late eclipses in the sun and moon." In *King Lear* nature is monstrous because man has been swallowed up in it:

A serving-man, proud in heart and mind; that curled my hair; wore gloves in my cap; served the lust of my mistress' heart and did the act of darkness with her; swore as many oaths as I spake words and broke them in the sweet face of heaven: one that slept in the contriving of lust and waked to do it: wine loved I deeply, dice dearly, and in woman out-paramoured the Turk: false of heart, light of ear, bloody of hand; hog in sloth, fox in stealth, wolf in greediness, dog in madness, lion in prey.

That is a picture of an animal with human faculties, made corrupt and legendary by the proudly curled hair. The conflict in Lear is a conflict between the sacred tradition of human society, which is old, and nature, which is always new, for it has no background. As I sat in that tramcar in Glasgow I was in an unhistorical world; I was outside time without being in eternity; in the small, sensual, momentary world of a beast.

But I believe that man has a soul and that it is immortal, not merely because on any other supposition human life would be inconceivable and monstrous; for I know that there are many people who believe that man is merely a thinking animal and yet do not consider him monstrous, and that there are a few people who, believing this, consider him monstrous, but do not find him inconceivable: who accept the nightmare and acknowledge nothing beyond it, as Swift did. But I think there are not many people who have the strength to do this; the great majority of those who see man as a thinking animal cannot do so without idealizing him, without seeing him ascending to some transcendent height in some future: they are sentimentalists with a passionate faith in self-help. My belief in immortality, so far as I can divine its origin, and that is not far, seems to be connected with the same impulse which urges me to know myself. I can never know myself; but the closer I come to knowledge of myself the more certain I must feel that I am immortal, and conversely, the more certain I am of my immortality the more intimately I must come to know myself. For I shall attend and listen to a class of experiences which the disbeliever in immortality ignores or dismisses as irrelevant to temporal life. The experiences I mean are of little practical use and have no particular economic or political interest. They come when I am least aware of myself as a personality moulded by my will and time: in moments of contemplation when I am unconscious of my body, or indeed that I have a body with separate members; in moments of grief or prostration; in happy hours with friends; and, because self-forgetfulness is most complete then, in dreams and daydreams and in that floating, half-discarnate state which precedes and follows sleep. In these hours there seems to me to be knowledge of my real self and simultaneously knowledge of immortality. Sleep tells us things both about ourselves and the world which we could not discover otherwise. Our dreams are part of experience; earlier ages acknowledged this. If I describe a great number of dreams in this book I do so intentionally, for I should like to save from the miscellaneous dross of experience a few glints of immortality.

I have had many dreams about animals, domestic, wild, and legendary, but I shall describe only one at this point, as it seems to me to throw into an imaginative

shape two of the things I have been writing about:
our relation to the animal world, a relation involving a
predestined guilt, and our immortality. All guilt seeks
expiation and the end of guilt, and our blood-guilti-
ness towards the animals tries to find release in visions
of a day when man and the beasts will live in friendship
and the lion will lie down with the lamb. My dream was
connected with this vision. I dreamed that I was lying
asleep, when a light in my room wakened me. A man
was standing by my bedside. He was wearing a long
robe, which fell about him in motionless folds, while
he stood like a column. The light that filled the room
came from his hair, which rose straight up from his
head, burning, like a motionless brazier. He raised his
hand, and without touching me, merely by making
that sign, lifted me to my feet in one movement, so
that I stood before him. He turned and went out
through the door, and I followed him. We were in the
gallery of a cloister; the moon was shining, and the
shadows of the arches made black ribs on the flag-
stones. We went through a street, at the end of which
there was a field, and while we walked on the moonlight changed to the white light of early morning. As
we passed the last houses I saw a dark, shabby man with
a dagger in his hand; he was wearing rags bound
round his feet, so that he walked quite soundlessly;
there was a stain as of blood on one of his sleeves;
I took him to be a robber or a murderer and was
afraid. But as he came nearer I saw that his eyes, which
were fixed immovably on the figure beside me, were
filled with a profound, violent adoration such as I had
never seen in human eyes before. Then, behind him, I

caught sight of a confused crowd of other men and
women in curious or ragged clothes, and all had their
eyes fixed with the same look on the man walking beside me. I saw their faces only for a moment. Presently
we came to the field, which as we drew near changed
into a great plain dotted with little conical hills a little
higher than a man's head. All over the plain animals
were standing or sitting on their haunches on these
little hills; lions, tigers, bulls, deer, elephants, were
there; serpents too wreathed their lengths on the
knolls; and each was separate and alone, and each
slowly lifted its head upward as if in prayer. This up-
ward-lifting motion had a strange solemnity and deli-
beration; I watched head after head upraised as if pro-
claiming some truth just realized, and yet as if moved
by an irresistible power beyond them. The elephant
wreathed its trunk upward, and there was something
pathetic and absurd in that indirect act of adoration.
But the other animals raised their heads with the in-
evitability of the sun's rising, as if they knew, like the
sun, that a new day was about to begin, and were
giving the signal for its coming. Then I saw a little
dog busily running about with his nose tied to the
ground, as if he did not know that the animals had been
redeemed. He was a friendly little dog, officiously
going about his business, and it seemed to me that he
too had a place in this day, and that his oblivious concern with the earth was also a sort of worship. How
the dream ended I do not remember: I have now only a
memory of the great animals with all their heads raised
to heaven.

I had this dream a long time after I left Orkney; I

was living in London and being psychoanalysed. I had so many dreams about this time that I could hardly keep count of them. In a great number of them I encountered dragons and mythological monsters, the explanation of the analyst being that I had for many years suppressed the animal in myself, so that it could come up now only in these wild and terrifying shapes. He was right up to a point in assuming this, for I had grown up a Puritan, and though I had liberated my mind, my senses were still bound. But he was right only up to a point, for the strange thing about these monsters was that they did not terrify me; instead I felt in a curious way at home with them. I can remember only one of them that frightened me: a great roaring sea-beast which I was trying to fight with an oar as I stood in a boat. I have had many dreams of fear, but except for this one hardly any of them have been connected with animals. It seems to me that most of the dreams I had about this time were ancestral dreams or Millennial dreams like the one I have just described. Our minds are possessed by three mysteries: where we came from, where we are going, and, since we are not alone, but members of a countless family, how we should live with one another. These questions are aspects of one question, and none of them can be separated from the others and dealt with alone. In my dream about the animals all three questions are involved; for the dream touches the relation between man and the animals and points to his origin, while in the image of the animal kingdom glorified and reconciled with mankind it points simultaneously to man's end, and with that to the way in which he should live

in a society, for that question is inseparable from the
question of his end.

From " An Autobiography"

---

*Dr Muir's reflection and imagination turn over the experi-
ence of boyhood and come to terms with it, drawing upon a
later wisdom. He looks at the modern world from outside,
as it were, and sees it very clearly and confidently. There is
religious faith behind his viewpoint; but more, those nourish-
ing early years in Orkney which led him to write of later
times: " The first few years after we came to Glasgow were
so stupidly wretched, such a meaningless waste of inherited
virtue, that I cannot write of them even now without grief
and anger."*

*Finding out about yourself truthfully is hard work.
Observe the range of memories and interests called upon
here: from Nietzsche the German poet-philosopher
through the Swift of "Gulliver's Travels" to the Shakespeare of "King Lear"; from Glasgow back to Orkney
and on to London; from the fruits of anthropological studies
to reflections about what men live for and why they are so
and not otherwise, and memories of dreams, and fragments
of particular experiences like the man in the tramcar,
made vivid by a poet's flair.*

*If this flair and this sensitiveness have made some
appeal, then Edwin Muir's "Collected Poems" (Faber
and Faber) will be worth exploring. If you are struck,
rather, by this kind of description and enquiry, the book
to find is Sir Herbert Read's "Annals of Innocence and
Experience" (Faber and Faber). It joins together "The
Innocent Eye," an account of a Yorkshire childhood, and
"In Retreat," in which the experiences of the First World
War shatter that earlier world.*

II

The Horror of War
1914-18

The Crash of Pillars
Edmund Blunden

Edmund Blunden served in France and Belgium with the Royal Sussex Regiment from 1916 to 1919, and he was awarded the Military Cross. His report upon the open horror and the degradation of war, and how it affected the sensitive and the vulnerable, is more softened by memory and by a natural dignity in the telling, than are the two that follow. Mr Blunden is a poet of some distinction, like Siegfried Sassoon and Robert Graves; but the urge to compose "Undertones of War" in prose came when he felt that his poetry had insufficiently uttered "the image and horror" of his war experiences. The book was first published some years after its completion, in 1928. It has appeared as a Penguin, but is not at present available in that form.

The Crash of Pillars is the title of this chapter: it describes an attack made in August 1917.

THE hour of attack had been fixed by the staff much earlier than the infantry wanted or thought suitable. The night had passed as such nights often do, shelling being less than was anticipated, silent altogether at times. I suppose it was about three when I shook hands with Colonel Millward, mounted the black-oozing steps of battle headquarters in the burrows below Bilge Street, and got into the assembly

ditch ("Hornby Trench") with my signallers. It was
thick darkness and slippery going, but we used an old
road part of the way. Where we lay, there were in the
darkness several tall tree-stumps above, and it felt like
a friendly ghost that watched the proceedings. A runner came round distributing our watches, which had
been synchronized at Bilge Street. At 3.50, if I am
right, shortly after Vidler had passed me growling
epigrams at some recent shellbursts which had covered
him with mud, the British guns spoke; a flooded
Amazon of steel flowed roaring, immensely fast, over
our heads, and the machine-gun bullets made a pattern
of sharper purpose and maniac language against that
diluvian rush. Flaring lights, small ones, great ones,
flew up and went spinning sideways in the cloud of
night; one's eyes seemed not quick enough; one heard
nothing from one's shouting neighbour, and only by
the quality of the noise and flame did I know that the
German shells crashing among the tree-stumps were
big ones and practically on top of us. We rose,
scrambled ahead, found No Man's Land a comparatively good surface, were amazed at the puny tags and
rags of once multiplicative German wire, and blundered over the once feared trench behind them without seeing that it was a trench. Good men as they were,
my party were almost all half-stunned by the unearthliness of our own barrage and when two were
wounded it was left to me to bandage them in my in-
effective way. (I have been reminded that two of our
party were killed, but at the time the fact was lost in
the insane unrealities all round.) The dark began to
dilute itself into daylight, and as went on we saw

concrete emplacements, apparently unattended to as yet, which had to be treated with care and suspicion; walking to the slanted low entrances with my revolver, I was well satisfied to prove them empty. And indeed the whole area seemed to be deserted! German dead, so obvious at every yard of a 1916 battlefield, were hardly to be seen. We still went ahead, and the mist whitened into dawn; through it came running a number of Germans—a momentary doubt; we prepared for a fight; no—"Prisoners!" shouted my batman. A minute more, and my advanced guard of signallers had come into touch with our companies, digging in by fours and fives along their captured objective. Meanwhile, I went ahead to see all that the mist allowed; there were troops of our Brigade advancing through the lines of men consolidating shellholes, and with map before me I could recognize some of the places which we had certainly captured. It seemed marvellous, for the moment. All ours—all these German trenches. Caliban Support, Calf Avenue, Calf Reserve. But, stay—even now a pity looks one in the face, for these trenches are mostly mere hedges of brushwood, hurdles, work for a sheepfold, with a shallow ditch behind; and they have been taking our weeks of gunfire in these!

The reflection and the sympathy actually occurred to me, but were soon obliterated by the day's work, and an increase in the German gunfire upon us. The slow twisting passage of the tanks through our position was thought to be the reason, for as these machines wheeled aside from the pits where our men were digging, heavy shells came down in plenty with formidable accuracy.

Besides, the enemy must have captured a set of operation maps with all the stages of advance displayed. I
remember that I was talking with somebody about one
"Charlie" Aston, an officer's servant, who had been
running here and there to collect watches from German
dead. He had just returned to his chosen shell-hole,
with several specimens, when a huge shell burst in the
very place. But not much notice was taken, or elegy
uttered, for everywhere the same instant destruction
threatened. And Tice and Collyer were already killed—
news as yet failing to have its full painfulness in the
thick of things.

The Battalion headquarters soon advanced from the
Old British front line, still conspicuous with the tall
tree-stumps, and crushed itself into a little concrete
dugout with a cupola over it, formerly used for a perfect survey of the British defences. I tried to throw up
enough earth to protect an annexe next door, but was
driven from the work by a machine-gun, hanging on
no great way off. Road-making parties had lost no
time and, strung out among the shellbursts, were
shovelling and pummelling tracks across old No Man's
Land. And then the Brigade headquarters came, beautiful to look upon, and their red tabs glowed out of
several shell-holes. This was more than the German
observers could endure, and in a short time there was
such a storm of high explosive on that small space that
the brains of the brigade withdrew, a trifle disillu-
sioned, to the old British trenches. Another storm, and
a more serious and incontestable one, was now creep-
ing on miserably with grey vapour of rain over the
whole field. It was one of the many which caused the

legend, not altogether dismissed even by junior officers, that the Germans could make it rain when they wanted to. Now, too, we were half certain that the attack had failed farther on, and one more brilliant hope, expressed a few hours before in shouts of joy, sank into the mud.

It was wet and it was cold. The marvel was that the day wore on, so heavy it was, and yet the day wore on and I found by my watch that it was afternoon. At battalion headquarters in the concrete look-out there were long faces, not in expression of despair but what is almost as bad—indefiniteness. In the doorway, where the wounds of several men were dressed, a man with a mortal wound in the back was propped up. This poor wretch again and again moaned, "I'm cold, cold," but seemed to have no other awareness of life. The doctor looked at him, and shook his head at me. A medical orderly looked at him and answered me he could do no good. I went out to visit company headquarters, which were now (with bombs and note-books) under waterproof sheets stretched over shell-holes, swiftly becoming swimming-baths. As the un-prepossessing evening came, N. C. Olive and myself were sharing a tin of "Sunshine" sausages in one of these pools.

The position grew no better during the night, and the succeeding day was dismal, noisy and horrid with sudden death. Tempers were not good, and I found myself suddenly threatening a sergeant-major with arrest for some unfriendly view which he was urging on the headquarters in general. Then, there were such incidents as the death of a runner called Rackley, a sensitive and willing youth, just as he set out for the companies; intercepted by a shrapnel bullet, he fell on one knee, and his stretched-out hand still clutched his message. Vidler, that invincible soldier, came in a little afterwards through explosions, observing, "That was a quick one, 'Erb. I was feeling round my backside for a few lumps of shrapnel—didn't find any though." This second day was on the whole drab in the extreme, and at the end of it we were ordered to relieve the 14th Hampshires in their position ahead, justly termed the Black Line, along the Steenbeck. The order presented no great intellectual difficulty, for our reduced battalion merely had to rise from its waterholes, plod through the mud of an already beaten track and crouch on the watch in other holes. Darkness clammy and complete, save for the flames of shells, masked that movement, but one stunted willow tree at which the track changed direction must haunt the memories of some of us. Trees in the battlefield are already described by Dante.

Headquarters—officers, signallers, servants, runners, and specialists—arrived in the blind gloom at the trench occupied by the Hampshire headquarters, and it is sufficient to indicate the insensate condition of the relief when I say that we did not notice any unusually close arrival of shells as we drew near to the trench, but as we entered it we found that there had just been one. It had blown in some concrete shelters, and killed and wounded several of our predecessors; I was aware of mummy-like half-bodies, and struggling figures, crying and cursing. Passing along towards the officers' dugout, we found the Hampshire colonel, sardonic and unshaken, who waited with us long hours while the

relief, so simple in the mention, so perplexing in the
midnight morass, was being completed. He told us that
in the daylight one only reached the front companies
through a machine gun barrage. He intended to have
taken out with him a German soft cap, but eventually
he forgot it; and perhaps I ought to be ashamed of
saying, that I have it to this day. It was the chief
museum-piece in the dugout, except for a stack of
German ration tobacco, which made a pretty comfortable seat. The smell of this little concrete hutch,
like all other German dugouts, was peculiar and heavy;
I do not know how they found the British lines, but
probably their experience would be parallel. It is a
matter which W. H. Hudson should have heard of,
when he was writing *A Hind in Richmond Park*.

The night spent itself somehow. Already it seemed
ages since I had last seen poor Tice, and looked at this
very patch of ground with him ("To give five ducats,
five, I would not farm it"), but the gulf between this
and three days before was indeed a black and lethal
abyss, which had swallowed up the hopes of the Allies
for this summer. I do not remember what was said.
Day brought a little promise of better weather, and
the guns were for a time quiet enough; I explored here
and there, and my signallers got their wires to "all
stations" into working order. A tank officer looked in,
asking help to salve some equipment from his wrecked
machine, lying just behind our pill-box. Presently the
drizzle was thronging down mistily again, and shelling
grew more regular and searching. There were a number of concrete shelters along the trench, and it was
not hard to see that their dispossessed makers were

determined to do them in. Our doctor, an Irishman named Gatchell, who seemed utterly to scorn such annoyances as Krupp, went out to find a much discussed bottle of whisky which he had left in his medical post. He returned, the bottle in his hand; "Now, you toping rascals"—a thump like a thunderbolt stopped him. He fell mute, white, face down, the bottle still in his hand; "Ginger" Lewis, the unshakable Adjutant, whose face I chanced to see particularly, went as chalky-white, and collapsed; the Colonel, shaking and staring, passed me as I stooped to pull the doctor out, and tottered, not knowing where he was going, along the trench. This was not surprising. Over my seat, at the entrance the direct hit had made a gash in the concrete, and the place was full of fragments and dust. The shell struck just over my head, and I suppose it was a 5·9. But we had escaped, and outside, scared from some shattered nook, a number of fieldmice were peeping and turning as though as puzzled as ourselves. A German listening-set with its delicate valves stood in the rain there, too, unfractured. But these details were perceived in a flash, and meanwhile shells were coming down remorselessly all along our alley. Other direct hits occurred, the Aid Post and the signallers' dugout were shattered. Men stood in the trench under their steel hats and capes resigned to their fate. I said to Sergeant Seall, "This is thick"; he tried to smile. A veterinary surgeon, Gatfield, with his droll, sleepy, profoundly kind manner, filled the doctor's place, and attended as best he could to the doctor and the other wounded. The continuous and ponderous blasts of shells seemed to me to imply that an attack was to be made on us, and being now more or less the only headquarters officer operating, after an inconclusive conference with the Colonel, I sent the S.O.S. to the artillery; the telephone wire went almost immediately afterwards. Our wonderful artillery answered, and at length the pulverization of our place slackened, to the relief of the starting nerves; whereon, Sergeant Ashford came to tell me that our linesmen had put us in touch with the 13th Royal Sussex on our right, and that the Adjutant of that battalion wanted me at the 'phone. Bartlett, a genial and gallant man, bright-haired Bartlett called me by name—I hear his self-control still in those telephoned words—and told me what made our own "direct hit" not worth mentioning. His headquarters had been pierced by a great shell, and over thirty killed or wounded. "A gunpit— Van Heule Farm"; I knew it by the map. What could we do to help? It was little enough; we called the R.A.M.C. to send rescuers to that gunpit, and I heard later that a driver actually succeeded in getting an ambulance to it, up the gouged and eruptioned St Julien Road.

The tragedy of the 13th came home to me more than all the rest, and from the moment of that telephone call my power of endurance lay gasping. Two chaplains visited us, to their glory and our pleasure, but not to our final comfort, for they brought no guess nor hint of our relief. One's range of effect, and of conception, seemed to close in, and the hole overhead in the resumed ill-smelling pillbox was ever catching the eye. I managed to fill in my diary for the day, and could not keep out some thoughts of better days. That night about twelve o'clock we were relieved ("all in billets by 3.30 A.M."), and even those who like myself had been for the last twenty-four hours in a gully or pit were scarcely able to credit it. Hobbling down the muddy muletrack, one found that the soles of one's feet had become corrugated, and the journey was desperately slow. No ordinary burst of shells could make us hurry now, but as we approached the dark earth wall of the Yser Canal, the notion of having a chance of escape quickened our dragging steps; and my own little group, passing a familiar spot called Irish Farm, went still quicker because of the most appalling missile we had ever heard. It was a high-velocity shell, and a big one; it came suddenly with a shriek beyond expression, entered the mud a few yards away, and rocked the earth and air. Perhaps the gunners were accustomed to this sort of nightmare, which in its solitary horror impressed me more even than the rolling storms of shell of the last few days.

The second-in-command, Frank Cassels, met us on the canal bank, and by his excellent household arrangements we got under cover there, and warmed ourselves with unforgettable, though very simple stew. Officers were herded together in a grimy dugout, with bunk beds; the men were in the long tunnels; and after a few hours of impervious sleep all woke to a sense of renewed misery. For one thing, we were expecting to be sent up again almost at once (the following night) into the battle. For another, a heavy battery in the field behind, next my old Red Hart Estaminet, was firing straight over our quarters, and at every discharge the roof of the dugout and our scalps seemed to be lifted and jarred with acute pain. Then, the desolate sky was still dropping rain, and the stricken landscape offered no relief. Two dumps of timber and ammunition flared and snapped along the transport track. In the tunnels the men were humbly dozing or cleaning up, one degree farther from the pale happiness of knowing "what it was all about" than we were. But that evening the Brigade-Major, Clark, who saw me going by his temporary "office," called me in for a word or two, in his usual tranquil tones disclosed some of the mistakes of the attack (our 15-inch artillery had fired for two hours on one of the positions already overrun by us, for example!) and told me the strange news that we were going out, the whole Division. I was sent ahead to seize enough tents for the battalion's accommodation.

Poperinghe again! even more divisional emblems, more badges and uniforms; more mud on the white house-fronts, more shutters up, fewer tiles on the roofs; the smell of petrol, veritably as sweet as life— we ask no violets yet. Through Poperinghe, among the wooden shops and taverns, to St Jans ter Biezen; a hopgarden or two, a shrine or two, peasants, dog-carts, poplars waving in the watery breeze. It is a real relief, but the battle has already become a vile and inglorious waste of our spirit; indeed to most of us it had from the first appeared a deal too ambitious, to vaunt it at Ypres. And even our pastoral retreat is now being visited at night by aircraft well accustomed to the art of murdering sleep if not life. Out of the line was out of the line in 1916, but we are older now.

From "Undertones of War"

"A vile and inglorious waste of our spirit": Mr Blunden's own phrase suggests the effect a report at once so brutal in its substance, and so firm and tender in its tone, makes upon us. But even the dereliction of the battle landscape called to mind the vision of Dante ("No green leaves but of dusky colour; no smooth boughs but knotted and warped; no fruit there but poisonous thorns"). Even during the ordeal he "could not keep out some thoughts of better days" and those thoughts provide him with a standpoint. Those who care to look into those thoughts more fully should go to his poetry (he has published three volumes, the last called "Shells by a Stream") and to books like "The Mind's Eye" and "English Villages." The best of his poems spring from a reticent, meditative sense of the English countryside; some of his war poems appear at the end of "Undertones of War," which has itself recently been published in the World's Classics series.

Out in No-man's-land
Siegfried Sassoon

*Siegfried Sassoon's " Memoirs of George Sherston" record,
under very thin disguises, the transition in his life from
secure, easy, and affluent country life to the front line in
France. At the outbreak of the War he was twenty-eight.
The story that followed was one of hectic bravery; of rebellion
against the War itself, the futility and the violence; of a
wounded officer's pacifist protest and its kindly masking by
officialdom under the term 'nervous breakdown'; of re-
cuperation, readjustment, and return for a brief period
to active service. But perhaps the clearest introduction to
Mr Sassoon is given in his colleague Robert Graves's book.
Here, especially: "I was told that Siegfried had distinguished himself by taking single-handed a battalion frontage
that the Royal Irish Regiment had failed to take the day
before. He had gone over with bombs in daylight, under
covering fire from a couple of rifles, and scared the occu-
pants out. It was a pointless feat; instead of reporting or
signalling for reinforcements he sat down in the German
trench and began dozing over a book of poems which he had
brought with him. When he finally went back he did not
report. The colonel was furious. The attack on Mametz
Wood had been delayed for two hours because it was reported
that British patrols were still out. 'British patrols' were
Siegfried and his book of poems. 'It would have got you a
D.S.O. if you'd only had more sense,' stormed the colonel.
Siegfried had been doing heroic things ever since I left the*

battalion. His nickname in the Seventh Division was ' Mad Jack.' He was given a Military Cross for bringing in a wounded lance corporal from a mine-crater close to the German lines, under heavy fire."

ON Saturday afternoon the order to move up took us by surprise. Two days of stagnation in the cramped little trench had relaxed expectancy, which now renewed itself in our compact preparations for departure. As usual on such occasions, the Company Sergeant-Major was busier than anybody else. I have probably said so before, but it cannot be too often repeated that C.S.M.'s were the hardest worked men in the infantry; everything depended on them, and if anyone deserved a K.C.B. it was a good C.S.M.

At 9 P.M. the Company fell in at the top of the ruined street of St Martin. Two guides from the outgoing battalion awaited us. We were to relieve some Northumberland Fusiliers in the Hindenburg Trench—the companies going up independently.

It was a grey evening, dry and windless. The village of St Martin was a shattered relic; but even in the devastated area one could be conscious of the arrival of spring, and as I took up my position in the rear of the moving column there was something in the sober twilight which could remind me of April evenings in England and the Butley cricket field where a few of us had been having our first knock at the nets. The cricket season had begun. . . . But the Company had left the shell-pitted road and was going uphill across open ground. Already the guides were making the pace too hot for the rear platoon; like most guides they were inconveniently nimble owing to their freedom from accoutrement, and insecurely confident that they knew the way. The muttered message "pass it along— steady the pace in front" was accompanied by the usual muffled clinkings and rattlings of arms and equipment. Unwillingly retarded, the guides led us into the deepening dusk. We hadn't more than two miles to go, but gradually the guides grew less authoritative. Several times they stopped to get their bearings. Leake fussed and fumed and they became more and more flurried. I began to suspect that our progress was circular.

At a midnight halt the hill still loomed in front of us; the guides confessed that they had lost their way, and Leake decided to sit down and wait for daylight. (There were few things more uncomfortable in the life of an officer than to be walking in front of a party of men all of whom knew that he was leading them in the wrong direction.) With Leake's permission I blundered experimentally into the gloom, fully expecting to lose both myself and the Company. By a lucky accident, I soon fell headlong into a sunken road and found myself among a small party of Sappers how could tell me where I was. It was a case of "Please, can you tell me the way to the Hindenburg Trench?" Congratulating myself on my cleverness I took one of the Sappers back to poor benighted B Company, and we were led to our Battalion rendezvous.

The rendezvous took some finding, since wrong map references had been issued by the Brigade Staff; but at last, after many delays, the Companies filed along to their ordained (and otherwise anathematized) positions.

We were at the end of a journey which had begun twelve days before, when we started from Camp 13. Stage by stage, we had marched to the life-denying region which from far away had threatened us with the blink and growl of its bombardments. Now we were groping and stumbling along a deep ditch to the place appointed for us in the zone of inhuman havoc. There must have been some hazy moonlight, for I remember the figures of men huddled against the sides of communication trenches; seeing them in some sort of ghastly glimmer (was it, perhaps, the diffused whiteness of a sinking flare beyond the ridge?), I was doubtful whether they were asleep or dead, for the attitudes of many were like death, grotesque and distorted. But this is nothing new to write about, you will say; just a weary company, squeezing past dead or drowsing men while it sloshes and stumbles to a front-line trench. Nevertheless that night relief had its significance for me, though in human experience it had been multiplied a millionfold. I, a single human being with my little stock of earthly experience in my head, was entering once again the veritable gloom and disaster of the thing called Armageddon. And I saw it then, as I see it now—a dreadful place, a place of horror and desolation which no imagination could have invented. Also it was a place where a man of strong spirit might know himself utterly powerless against death and destruction, and yet stand up and defy gross darkness and stupefying shell-fire, discovering in himself the invincible resistance of an animal or an insect, and an endurance which he might, in after days, forget or disbelieve.

Anyhow, there I was, leading that little procession of Flintshire Fusiliers many of whom had never seen a frontline trench before. At that juncture they asked no compensation for their efforts except a mug of hot tea. The tea would have been a miracle, and we didn't get it till next morning but there was some comfort in the fact that it wasn't raining.

It was nearly four o'clock when we found ourselves in the Hindenburg Main Trench. After telling me to post the sentries, Leake disappeared down some stairs to the Tunnel (which will be described later on). The Company we were relieving had already departed, so there was no one to give me any information. At first I didn't even know for certain that we were in the Front Line. The trench was a sort of gully, deep, wide, and unfinished looking. The sentries had to clamber up a bank of loose earth before they could see over the top. Our Company was only about eighty strong and its sector was fully 600 yards. The distance between the sentry-posts made me aware of our inadequacy in that wilderness. I had no right to feel homeless, but I did; and if I had needed to be reminded of my forlorn situation as a living creature I could have done it merely by thinking of a Field Cashier. Fifty franc notes were comfortable things, but they were no earthly use up here, and the words "Field Cashier" would have epitomized my remoteness from smugness and security, and from all assurance that I should be alive and kicking the week after next. But it would soon be Sunday morning; such ideas weren't wholesome, and there was a certain haggard curiosity attached to the proceedings; combined with the self-dramatizing desperation which enabled a good many of us to worry our way through much worse emergencies than mine.

When I had posted the exhausted sentries, with as much cheeriness as I could muster, I went along to look for the Company on our left. Rather expecting to find one of our own companies, I came round a corner to a place where the trench was unusually wide. There I found myself among a sort of panic party which I was able to identify as a platoon (thirty or forty strong). They were jostling one another in their haste to get through a cavernous doorway, and as I stood astonished one of them breathlessly told me that "the Germans were coming over." Two officers were shepherding them downstairs and before I'd had time to think the whole lot had vanished. The Battalion they belonged to was one of those amateur ones which were at such a disadvantage owing to lack of discipline and the absence of trained N.C.O.'s. Anyhow, their behaviour seemed to indicate that the Tunnel in the Hindenburg Trench was having a lowering effect on their morale.

Out in no-man's-land there was no sign of any German activity. The only remarkable thing was the unbroken silence. I was in a sort of twilight, for there was a moony glimmer in the low-clouded sky; but the unknown territory in front was dark, and I stared out at it like a man looking from the side of a ship. Returning to my own sector I met a runner with a verbal message from Battalion H.Q. B Company's front was to be thoroughly patrolled at once. Realizing the futility of sending any of my few spare men out on patrol (they'd been walking about for seven hours and were dead beat) I lost my temper, quietly and inwardly. Shirley and Rees were nowhere to be seen and it wouldn't have been fair to send them out, inexperienced as they were. So I stumped along to our right-flank post, told them to pass it along that a patrol was going out from right to left, and then started sulkily out for a solitary stroll in no-man's-land. I felt more annoyed with Battalion Headquarters than with the enemy. There was no wire in front of the trench, which was, of course, constructed for people facing the other way. I counted my steps, 200 steps straight ahead; then I began to walk the presumptive 600 steps to the left. But it isn't easy to count your steps in the dark among shell-holes, and after a problematic 400 I lost confidence in my automatic pistol, which I was grasping in my right-hand breeches pocket. Here I am, I thought, alone out in this god-forsaken bit of ground, with quite a good chance of bumping into a Boche strong-post. Apparently there was only one reassuring action which I could perform; so I expressed my opinion of the War by relieving myself (for it must be remembered that there are other reliefs beside Battalion reliefs). I ensured my sense of direction by placing my pistol on the ground with its muzzle pointing the way I was going. Feeling less lonely and afraid, I finished my patrol without having met so much as a dead body, and regained the trench exactly opposite our left-hand post, after being huskily challenged by an irresolute sentry, who, as I realized at the time, was the greatest danger I had encountered. It was now just beginning to be more daylight than darkness, and when I stumbled down a shaft to the underground trench I left the sentries shivering under a red and rainy-looking sky.

There were fifty steps down the shaft; the earthy smell of that triumph of Teutonic military engineering was strongly suggestive of appearing in the Roll of Honour and being buried until the Day of Judgment. Dry-mouthed and chilled to the bone, I lay in a wire-netting bunk and listened to the dismal snorings of my companions. Along the Tunnel the air blew deathly cold and seasoned with mephitic odours. In vain I envied the snorers; but I was getting accustomed to lack of sleep, and three hours later I was gulping some peculiar tea with morose enjoyment. Owing to the scarcity of water (which had to be brought up by the Transport who were eight miles back, at Blairville) washing wasn't possible; but I contrived a refreshing shave, utilizing the dregs of my tea.

By ten o'clock I was above ground again, in charge of a fatigue party. We went half-way back to St Martin, to an ammunition dump, whence we carried up boxes of trench mortar bombs. I carried a box myself, as the conditions were vile and it seemed the only method of convincing the men that it had to be done. We were out nearly seven hours; it rained all day and the trenches were a morass of glue-like mud. The unmitigated misery of that carrying party was a typical infantry experience of discomfort without actual danger. Even if the ground had been dry the boxes would have been too heavy for most of the men; but we were lucky in one way; the wet weather was causing the artillery to spend an inactive Sunday. It was a yellow corpse-like day, more like November than April, and the landscape was desolate and treeless. What we were doing was quite unexceptional; millions of soldiers endured the same sort of thing and got badly shelled into the bargain. Nevertheless I can believe that my party, staggering and floundering under its loads, would have made an impressive picture of "Despair." The background, too, was appropriate. We were among the debris of the intense bombardment of ten days before, for we were passing along and across the Hindenburg Outpost Trench, with its belt of wire (fifty yards in places); here and there these rusty jungles had been flattened by tanks. The Outpost Trench was about 200 yards from the Main Trench, which was now our front line. It had been solidly made, ten feet deep, with timbered fire-steps, splayed sides, and timbered steps at intervals to front and rear and to machine-gun emplacements. Now it was wrecked as though by earthquake and eruption. Concrete strong-posts were smashed, and tilted sideways; everywhere the chalky soil was pocked and pitted with huge shell-holes; and wherever we looked the mangled effigies of the dead were our *memento mori*. Shell-twisted and dismembered, the Germans maintained the violent attitudes in which they had died. The British had mostly been killed by bullets or bombs, so they looked more resigned. But I can remember a pair of hands (nationality unknown) which protruded from the soaked ashen soil like the roots of a tree turned upside down; one hand seemed to be pointing at the sky with an accusing gesture. Each time I passed that place the protest of those fingers became more expressive of an appeal to God in defiance of those who made the War. Who made the War? I laughed hysterically as the thought passed through my mud-stained mind. But I only laughed mentally, for my box of Stokes gun ammunition left me no breath to spare for an angry guffaw. And the dead were the dead; this was no time to be pitying them or asking silly questions about their outraged lives. Such sights must be taken for granted, I thought, as I gasped and slithered and stumbled with my disconsolate crew. Floating on the surface of the flooded trench was the mask of a human face which had detached itself from the skull.

Plastered with mud and soaked to the skin, the fatigue-party clumped down the steps to the Tunnel. The carrying job was finished; but a stimulating surprise awaited me, for Leake was just back from Battalion H.Q. (somewhere along the Tunnel) and he breezily informed me that I'd been detailed to take command of a hundred bombers in the attack which had been arranged for next morning. "Twenty-five bombers from each Company; you're to act as reserve for the Cameronians," he remarked. I stared at him over my mug of reviving but trench-flavoured tea (made with chlorinated water) and asked him to tell me some more. He said: "Well, they're a bit hazy about it at Headquarters, but the General is frightfully keen on our doing an underground attack along the Tunnel, as well as along the main trench up above. You've got to go and discuss the tactical situation with one of the Company commanders up in the Front Line on our right." All that I knew about the tactical situation was that if one went along the Tunnel one arrived at a point where a block had been made by blowing it in. On the other side one bumped into the Germans. Above ground there was a barrier and the situation was similar. Bombing along a Tunnel in the dark. . . . Had the War Office issued a text book on the subject? . . . I lit my pipe, but failed to enjoy it, probably because the stewed tea had left such a queer taste in my mouth.

Ruminating on the comfortless responsibility imposed on me by this enterprise, I waited until nightfall. Then a superbly cheerful little guide bustled me along a maze of waterlogged ditches until I found myself in a small dug-out with some friendly Scotch officers and a couple of flame-wagging candles. The dug-out felt more like old times than the Hindenburg Tunnel, but the officers made me feel incompetent and uninformed, for they were loquacious about local trench topography which meant nothing to my newly-arrived mind. So I puffed out my Military Cross ribbon (the dug-out contained two others), nodded my head knowingly, and took an acquiescent share in the discussion of the strategic situation. Details of organization were offered me and I made a few smudgy notes. The Cams didn't think that there was much chance of my party being called on to support them, and they were hoping that the underground attack would be eliminated from operation orders.

I emerged from the desperation jollity of their little den with only a blurred notion of what it was all about. The objective was to clear the trench for 500 yards

while other battalions went over the top on our left
to attack Fontaine-les-Croiselles. But I was, at the best
of times, only an opportunist officer; technical talk in
the Army always made me feel mutely inefficient. And
now I was floundering home in the dark to organize
my command, put something plausible on paper, and
take it along to the Adjutant. If only I could consult
the Doctor, I thought; for he was back from leave,
though I hadn't seen him yet. It seemed to me, in my
confused and exhausted condition, that I was at a crisis
in my military career; and, as usual, my main fear was
that I should make a fool of myself. The idea of making
a fool of oneself in that murderous mix-up now
appears to me rather a ludicrous one; for I see myself
merely as a blundering flustered little beetle; and if
someone happens to put his foot on a beetle, it is unjust to accuse the unlucky insect of having made a fool
of itself. When I got back to Leake and Rees and
Shirley I felt so lost and perplexed that I went straight
on to Battalion H.Q.

The Tunnel was a few inches higher than a tall man
walking upright; it was fitted with bunks and recessed
rooms; in places it was crowded with men of various
units, but there were long intervals of unwholesome-
smelling solitude. Prying my way along with an electric
torch, I glimpsed an assortment of vague shapes, boxes,
tins, fragments of broken furniture and frowsy mat-
tresses. It seemed a long way to Headquarters, and the
Tunnel was memorable but not fortifying to a fatigued
explorer who hadn't slept for more than an hour at a
stretch or taken his clothes off since last Tuesday.
Once, when I tripped and recovered myself by grabbing

the wall, my tentative patch of brightness revealed somebody half hidden under a blanket. Not a very clever spot to be taking a nap, I thought as I stooped to shake him by the shoulder. He refused to wake up, so I gave him a kick. "God blast you, where's Battalion Headquarters?" My nerves were on edge; and what right had he to be having a good sleep, when I never seemed to get five minutes' rest? . . . Then my beam settled on the livid face of a dead German whose fingers still clutched the blackened gash on his neck. . . . Stumbling on, I could only mutter to myself that this was really a bit too thick. (That, however, was an exaggeration; there is nothing remarkable about a dead body in a European War, or a squashed beetle in a cellar.) At Headquarters I found the Adjutant alone, worried and preoccupied with clerical work. He had worked in an office, at accountancy, I believe, before the War; and now most of his fighting was done in writing, though he had served his apprenticeship as a brave and indefatigable platoon commander. He told me that the underground attack had been washed out by a providential counter-order from Division, and asked me to send my organization scheme along as soon as possible. "Right-O!" I replied, and groped my way back again feeling the reverse of my reply. By a stroke of luck I discovered Ralph Wilmot, sitting by himself in a small recessed room—his dark hair smoothly brushed and his countenance pensive but unperturbed. He might conceivably have been twiddling a liqueur glass in a Piccadilly restaurant. Unfortunately he had no liquid refreshment to offer, but his philosophic way of greeting me was a consolation and in him I confided my dilemma. With an understanding air he assumed his monocle, deliberated for a while, snuffed the candle wick, and wrote out an authoritative looking document headed "Organization of F.F. Parties." The gist of it was "15 Bombers (each carrying 5 grenades). 5 Carriers (also act as bayonet men). 1 Full Rank." There wasn't much in it, he remarked, as he appended "a little bit of skite about consolidation and defensive flanks." It certainly looked simple enough when it was done, though I had been at my wits' end about it.

While he was fixing up my future for me I gazed around and thought what a queer refuge I'd found for what might possibly be my final night on earth. Dugout though it was, the narrow chamber contained a foggy mirror and a clock. The clock wasn't ticking, but its dumb face stared at me, an idiot reminder of real rooms and desirable domesticity. Outside the doorless doorway people were continually passing in both directions with a sound of shuffling feet and mumbling voices. I caught sight of a red-capped Staff Officer, and a party of sappers carrying picks and shovels. The Tunnel was a sort of highway and the night had brought a considerable congestion of traffic. When we'd sent my document along to the Adjutant there was nothing more to be done except sit and wait for operation orders. It was now about ten o'clock.

As evidence of my own soldierly qualities I would like to be able to declare that we eagerly discussed every aspect of the situation as regards next morning's attack. But the truth is that we said nothing at all about it. The thing had to be attempted and there was an end of it (until zero hour). The Brigadier and his

Staff (none too bright at map-references) were hoping to satisfy (vicariously) General Whincop (who'd got an unpopular bee in his bonnet about the Rum Ration, and had ordered an impossible raid, two months ago, which had been prevented by a providential thaw and caused numerous deaths in a subsequently sacrificed battalion).

Whincop was hoping to satisfy the Corps Commander, of whom we knew nothing at all, except that he had insulted our Colonel on the Doullens road. The Corps Commander hoped to satisfy the Army Commander, who had as usual informed us that we were "pursuing a beaten enemy," and who had brought the Cavalry up for a "break-through." (It is worth mentioning that the village which was now our Division's objective was still held by the Germans eight months afterwards.) And the Army Commander, I suppose, was in telephonic communication with the Commander-in-Chief, who, with one eye on Marshal Foch, was hoping to satisfy his King and Country. Such being the case, Wilmot and myself were fully justified in leaving the situation to the care of the military caste who were making the most of their Great Opportunity for obtaining medal-ribbons and reputations for leadership; and if I am being caustic and captious about them I can only plead the need for a few minutes' post-war retaliation. Let the Staff write their own books about the Great War, say I. The Infantry were biased against them, and their authentic story will be read with interest.

As for our conversation between ten o'clock and midnight (when my operation orders arrived from the

Adjutant) I suppose it was a form of drug, since it was
confined to pleasant retrospections of peace. Wilmot
was well acquainted with my part of the world and
he'd come across many of our local worthies. So we
were able to make a little tour of the Kentish Weald
and the Sussex border, as though on a couple of
mental bicycles. In imagination we cycled along on a
fine summer afternoon, passing certain milestones
which will always be inseparable from my life history.
Outside Squire Maundle's park gate we shared a distinct picture of his angular attitudes while he addressed
his golf-ball among the bell-tinklings and baaings of
sheep on the sunny slopes above Amblehurst (always
followed by a taciturn black retriever). Much has been
asserted about the brutalized conditions of mind to
which soldiers were reduced by life in the Front Line;
I do not deny this, but I am inclined to suggest that
there was a proportionate amount of simple-minded
sentimentality. As far as I was concerned, no topic
could be too homely for the trenches.

Thus, while working parties and machine-gunners
filed past the door with hollow grumbling voices, our
private recess in the Hindenburg Tunnel was pre-
cariously infused with evocations of rural England and
we challenged our surroundings with remembrances
of parish names and farm-houses with friendly faces.
A cottage garden was not an easy idea to recover con-
vincingly. . . . Bees among yellow wallflowers on a
warm afternoon. The smell of an apple orchard in
autumn. . . . Such details were beyond our evocation.
But they were implied when I mentioned Squire
Maundle in his four-wheeled dogcart, rumbling along

the Dumbridge Road to attend a County Council
meeting.

"*Secret*. The Bombing Parties of 25 men will rendezvous at 2.30 A.M. tomorrow morning, 16th inst. in
shafts near C Coy. H.Q. The greatest care will be
taken that each separate Company Party keeps to one
side of the Shaft and that the Dump of Bombs be in
the trench at the head of these shafts, suitably split.
The necessity of keeping absolute silence must be
impressed on all men. These parties (under 2nd Lt.
Sherston) will come under the orders of O.C. Cameronians at ZERO minus 10. Lt. Dunning and 2 orderlies
will act liaison and report to O.C. Cameronians at
ZERO minus 5. While the parties are in the shaft
they must keep a free passage way clear for runners,
etc."

Such was the document which (had I been less fortunate) would have been my passport to the Stygian
shore. In the meantime, with another two hours to sit
through, we carried on with our world without end
conversation. We were, I think, on the subject of
Canterbury Cricket Week when my watch warned me
that I must be moving on. As I got up from the table
on which we'd been leaning our elbows, a blurred
version of my face looked at me from the foggy mirror
with an effect of clairvoyance. Hoping that this was an
omen of survival, I went along to the rendezvous-
shaft and satisfied myself that the Bombing Parties
were sitting on the stairs in a bone-chilling draught,
with my two subordinate officers in attendance.

Zero hour was at 3 A.M. and the prefatory uproar

was already rumbling overhead. Having tightened my mud-caked puttees and put my tie straight (there was no rule against wearing a tie in an attack) diffidently I entered the Cameronian H.Q. dug-out, which was up against the foot of the stairs. I was among strangers, and Zero minus 10 wasn't a time for conversational amenities, so I sat self-consciously while the drumming din upstairs was doing its utmost to achieve a reassuring climax. Three o'clock arrived. The tick-tacking telephone-orderly in a corner received a message that the attack had started. They were over the barrier now, and bombing up the trench. The Cameronian Colonel and his Adjutant conversed in the constrained undertones of men who expect disagreeable news. The Colonel was a fine-looking man, but his well-disciplined face was haggard with anxiety. Dunning sat in another corner, serious and respectful, with his natural jollity ready to come to the surface whenever it was called for.

At the end of twenty minutes' tension the Colonel exclaimed abruptly, "Good God, I wish I knew how they're doing! . . ." And then, as if regretting his manifestation of feeling, "No harm in having a bit of cake, anyhow." There was a large home-made cake on the table. I was offered a slice, which I munched with embarrassment. I felt that I had no business to be there at all, let alone helping to make a hole in the Colonel's cake, which was a jolly good one. I couldn't believe that these competent officers were counting on me to be of any use to them if I were required to take an active part in the proceedings upstairs. Then the telephone-orderly announced that communication with

Captain Macnair's headquarters had broken down;
after that the suspense continued monotonously. I had
been sitting there about two and a half hours when it
became evident that somebody was descending the
steps in a hurry. H.Q. must have kept its cooking
utensils on the stairs, for the visitor arrived outside the
doorway in a clattering cascade of pots and pans. He
was a breathless and dishevelled sergeant, who blurted
out an incoherent statement about their having been
driven back after advancing a short distance. While the
Colonel questioned him in a quiet and controlled voice
I rose stiffly to my feet. I don't remember saying anything or receiving any orders; but I felt that the
Cameronian officers were sensitive to the delicacy of
my situation. There was no question of another slice
of home-made cake. Their unuttered comment was,
"Well, old chap, I suppose you're for it now."

Leaving them to get what satisfaction they could
from the sergeant's story, I grinned stupidly at Dunning, popped my helmet on my head, and made for the
stairway. It must have been a relief to be doing something definite at last, for without pausing to think I
started off with the section of twenty-five who were
at the top of the stairs. Sergeant Baldock got them on
the move at once, although they were chilled and
drowsy after sitting there for over three hours. None
of them would have been any the worse for a mouthful
of rum at that particular moment. In contrast to the
wearisome candlelight of the lower regions, the out-
door world was bright and breezy; animated also by
enough noise to remind me that some sort of battle
was going on. As we bustled along the flustered little

contingent at my heels revived from its numbness.
I had no idea what I was going to do; our destination
was in the brain of the stooping Cameronian guide
who trotted ahead of me. On the way we picked up a
derelict Lewis gun, which I thought might come in
handy though there was no ammunition with it. At the
risk of being accused of "taking the wrong half of the
conversation" (a favourite phrase of Aunt Evelyn's)
I must say that I felt quite confident. (Looking back
on that emergency from my arm-chair, I find some
difficulty in believing that I was there at all.) For about
ten minutes we dodged and stumbled up a narrow
winding trench. The sun was shining; large neutral
clouds voyaged willingly with the wind; I felt intensely
alive and rather out of breath. Suddenly we came into
the main trench, and where it was widest we met the
Cameronians. I must have picked up a bomb on the
way, for I had one in my hand when I started my conversation with young Captain Macnair. Our encounter
was more absurd than impressive. Macnair and his
exhausted men were obviously going in the wrong
direction, and I was an incautious newcomer. Consequently I had the advantage of him while he told me
that the Germans were all round them and they'd run
out of bombs. Feeling myself to be, for the moment,
an epitome of Flintshire infallibility, I assumed an air
of jaunty unconcern; tossing my bomb carelessly from
left hand to right and back again, I inquired, "But
where *are* the Germans?"—adding, "I can't see any of
them." This effrontery had its effect (though for some
reason I find it difficult to describe this scene without
disliking my own behaviour). The Cameronian officers

looked around them and recovered their composure. Resolved to show them what intrepid reinforcements we were, I assured Macnair that he needn't worry any more and we'd soon put things straight. I then led my party past his, halted them, and went up the trench with Sergeant Baldock—an admirably impassive little man who never ceased to behave like a perfectly trained and confidential man-servant. After climbing over some sort of barricade, we went about fifty yards without meeting anyone. Observing a good many Mills' bombs lying about in little heaps, I sent Baldock back to have them collected and carried further up the trench. Then, with an accelerated heart beat, I went round the corner by myself. Unexpectedly, a small man was there, standing with his back to me, stockstill and watchful, a haversack of bombs slung over his left shoulder. I saw that he was a Cameronian corporal; we did not speak. I also carried a bag of bombs; we went round the next bay. There my adventurous ardour experienced a sobering shock. A fair-haired Scotch private was lying at the side of the trench in a pool of his own blood. His face was grey and serene, and his eyes stared emptily at the sky. A few yards further on the body of a German officer lay crumpled up and still. The wounded Cameronian made me feel angry, and I slung a couple of bombs at our invisible enemies, receiving in reply an egg bomb, which exploded harmlessly behind me. After that I went bombing busily along, while the corporal (more artful and efficient than I was) dodged in and out of the saps—a precaution which I should have forgotten. Between us we created quite a demonstration of offensiveness, and in this manner arrived at our objective without getting more than a few glimpses of retreating field-grey figures. I had no idea where our objective was, but the corporal informed me that we had reached it, and he seemed to know his business. This, curiously enough, was the first time either of us had spoken since we met.

The whole affair had been so easy that I felt like pushing forward until we bumped into something more definite. But the corporal had a cooler head and he advised discretion. I told him to remain where he was and started to explore a narrow sap on the left side of the trench. (Not that it matters whether it was on the left side or the right, but it appears to be the only detail I can remember; and when all is said and done, the War was mainly a matter of holes and ditches.) What I expected to find along that sap, I can't say. Finding nothing, I stopped to listen. There seemed to be a lull in the noise of the attack along the line. A few machine-guns tapped, spiteful and spasmodic. High up in the fresh blue sky an aeroplane droned and glinted. I thought what a queer state of things it all was, and then decided to take a peep at the surrounding country. This was a mistake which ought to have put an end to my terrestrial adventures, for no sooner had I popped my silly head out of the sap than I felt a stupendous blow in the back between my shoulders. My first notion was that a bomb had hit me from behind, but what had really happened was that I had been sniped from in front. Anyhow my foolhardy attitude toward the Second Battle of the Scarpe had been instantaneously altered for the worse. I leant against the side of the sap and shut my eyes. . . . When I reopened them

Sergeant Baldock was beside me, discreet and sympathetic, and to my surprise I discovered that I wasn't dead. He helped me back to the trench, gently investigated my wound, put a field-dressing on it, and left me sitting there while he went to bring up some men.

After a short spell of being deflated and sorry for myself, I began to feel rabidly heroical again, but in a slightly different style, since I was now a wounded hero, with my arm in a superfluous sling. All my seventy-five men were now on the scene (minus a few who had been knocked out by our own shells, which were dropping short). I can remember myself talking volubly to a laconic Stokes-gun officer, who had appeared from nowhere with his weapon and a couple of assistants. I felt that I must make one more onslaught before I turned my back on the War and my only idea was to collect all available ammunition and then renew the attack while the Stokes-gun officer put up an enthusiastic barrage. It did not occur to me that anything else was happening on Allenby's Army Front except my own little show. My over-strained nerves had wrought me up to such a pitch of excitement that I was ready for any suicidal exploit. This convulsive energy might have been of some immediate value had there been any objective for it. But there was none; and before I had time to inaugurate anything rash and irrelevant Dunning arrived to relieve me. His air of competent unconcern sobered me down, but I was still inflamed with the offensive spirit and my impetuosity was only snuffed out by a written order from the Cameronian Colonel, who forbade any further advance

owing to the attack having failed elsewhere. My fero-
city fizzled out then, and I realized that I had a raging
thirst. As I was starting my return journey (I must have
known then that nothing could stop me till I got to
England) the M.O. came sauntering up the trench with
the detached demeanour of a gentle botanist. "Trust
him to be up there having a look round," I thought.
Within four hours of leaving it I was back in the
Tunnel.

Back at Battalion Headquarters in the Tunnel I
received from our Colonel and Adjutant generous con-
gratulations on my supposedly dashing display. In the
emergency candlelight of that draughty cellar recess I
bade them good-bye with voluble assurances that I
should be back in a few weeks; but I was so over-
strained and excited that my assurances were noises
rather than notions. Probably I should have been
equally elated without my wound; but if unwounded,
I'd have been still up at the Block with the bombing
parties. In the meantime, nothing that happened to me
could relieve Battalion H.Q. of its burdens. The Adjutant would go on till he dropped, for he had an inex-
haustible sense of duty. I never saw him again; he was
killed in the autumn up at Ypres. . . . I would like to
be able to remember that I smiled grimly and departed
reticently. But the "bombing show" had increased my
self-importance, and my exodus from the Front Line
was a garrulous one. A German bullet had passed
through me leaving a neat hole near my right shoulder-
blade and this patriotic perforation had made a different man of me. I now looked at the War, which had

been a monstrous tyrant, with liberated eyes. For the time being I had regained my right to call myself a private individual.

The first stage of my return journey took me to the Advanced Dressing Station at Henin. My servant went with me, carrying my haversack. He was a quiet clumsy middle-aged man who always did his best and never complained. While we picked our way along the broken ground of Henin Hill I continued talkative, halting now and again to recover breath and take a last stare at the blighted slope where yesterday I had stumbled to and fro with my working party.

The sky was now overcast and the landscape grey and derelict. The activities of the attack had subsided, and we seemed to be walking in a waste land where dead men had been left out in the rain after being killed for no apparent purpose. Here and there, figures could be seen moving toward the Dressing Station, some of them carrying stretchers.

It was the midday stagnation which usually followed an early morning attack. The Dressing Station was a small underground place crowded with groaning wounded. Two doctors were doing what they could for men who had paid a heavy price for their freedom. My egocentricity diminished among all that agony. I remember listening to an emotional padre who was painfully aware that he could do nothing except stand about and feel sympathetic. The consolations of the Church of England weren't much in demand at an Advance Dressing Station. I was there myself merely to go through the formality of being labelled "walking wounded." I was told to go on to a place called "B.

Echelon," which meant another three miles of muddy walking. Beat to the world, I reached B. Echelon, and found our Quartermaster in a tent with several officers newly arrived from the Base and one or two back from leave. Stimulated by a few gulps of whisky and water, I renewed my volubility and talked nineteen to the dozen until the kind Quartermaster put me into the mess-cart which carried me to a cross road where I waited for a motor bus. There, after a long wait, I shook hands with my servant, and the handshake seemed to epitomize my good-bye to the Second Battalion. I thanked him for looking after me so well; but one couldn't wish a man luck when he was going back to the Hindenburg Trench. It may be objected that my attitude toward the Western Front was too intimate; but this was a question of two human beings, one of whom was getting out of it comfortably while the other went back to take his chance in the world's worst war. . . . In the bus, wedged among "walking wounded," I was aware that I had talked quite enough. For an hour and a half we bumped and swayed along ruined roads till we came to the Casualty Clearing Station at Warlencourt. It was seven o'clock and all I got that night was a cup of Bovril and an anti-tetanus injection.

The place was overcrowded with bad cases and I had to wait until after midnight for a bed. I remember sitting in a chair listening to the rain pelting on the roof of the tent and the wailing of a wintry wind. I was too exhausted to sleep; my head had lost control of its thoughts, which continued to re-echo my good-bye garrulities; the injection had made me feel chilly and queer, and my wound began to be painful. But I was able to feel sorry for "the poor old Battalion" (which was being relieved that night) and to be thankful for my own lucky escape.

What I'd been through was nothing compared with the sort of thing that many soldiers endured over and over again; nevertheless I condoled with myself on having had no end of a bad time.

Next afternoon a train (with 500 men and 35 officers on board) conveyed me to a Base Hospital. My memories of that train are strange and rather terrible, for it carried a cargo of men in whose minds the horrors they had escaped from were still vitalized and violent. Many of us still had the caked mud of the war zone on our boots and clothes, and every bandaged man was accompanied by his battle experience. Although many of them talked lightly and even facetiously about it, there was an aggregation of enormities in the atmosphere of that train. I overheard some slightly wounded officers who were excitedly remembering their adventures up at Wancourt, where they'd been bombed out of a trench in the dark. Their jargoning voices mingled with the rumble and throb of the train as it journeyed —so safely and sedately—through the environing gloom. The Front Line was behind us; but it could lay its hand on our hearts, though its bludgeoning reality diminished with every mile. It was as if we were pursued by the Arras Battle which had now become a huge and horrible idea. We might be boastful or sagely reconstructive about our experience, in accordance with our different characters. But our minds were still out of breath and our inmost thoughts in disorderly retreat from bellowing darkness and men dying out in shell-holes under the desolation of returning daylight. We were the survivors; few among us would ever tell the truth to our friends and relations in England. We were carrying something in our heads which belonged to us alone, and to those we had left behind us in the battle. There were dying men, too, on board that Red Cross train, men dying for their country in comparative comfort.

We reached our destination after midnight, and the next day I was able to write in my diary: "I am still feeling warlike and quite prepared to go back to the Battalion in a few weeks; I am told that my wound will be healed in a fortnight. The doctor here says I am a lucky man as the bullet missed my jugular vein and spine by a fraction of an inch. I know it would be better for me not to go back to England, where I should probably be landed for at least three months and then have all the hell of returning again in July or August." But in spite of my self-defensive scribble I was in London on Friday evening, and by no means sorry to be carried through the crowd of patriotic spectators at Charing Cross Station. My stretcher was popped into an ambulance which took me to a big hospital at Denmark Hill. At Charing Cross a woman handed me a bunch of flowers and a leaflet by the Bishop of London who earnestly advised me to lead a clean life and attend Holy Communion.

From "Memoirs of an Infantry Officer"

That narrative came from the chapter called 'The Second Battalion' in "Memoirs of an Infantry Officer." The pain, the brutality, are more vivid here, and the conscious self of the writer, struggling, suffering, surviving, feels intensely close. He shows no self-pity, no self-indulgence; the horror and the madness of it all go very deep and they cannot be altogether controlled, but the effort of the prose is to be as honest as possible. The note of desperation is never far off, and memories of decent living are a way of holding on to sanity.

Mr Sassoon is justly known as much for his passionate and bitter war poems, as for the "Memoirs." But there is a gentler side to his poetic talent, and "Poems, Newly Selected" (Faber and Faber) gives a fair view of his range. Equally, there is a gentler side to the "Memoirs" and it dominates the final volume, "Sherston's Progress."

Triste, La Guerre
Robert Graves

*Like Mr Sassoon, Robert Graves served with the Royal
Welch Fusiliers. These two passages from "Good-bye
to All That" produce an even more painful impression of
squalid catastrophe. It comes out most sharply in the discrepancy between what is said, and the way it is said. The
detail is brutal, unsoftened, and unadorned; the whole report seems alive with veracity. Yet the tone of voice is
matter-of-fact, or wry, or curt and abrupt, or mocking.
More than Mr Sassoon, Mr Graves has his dreadful
experiences firmly under control; he has given them distance
and perspective: but it has cost a lot, and you can feel the
strain. Observe too how differently he suggests the thin
connexion with a more humane world. He refers not to his
thoughts, or to happier memories used like an anaesthetic,
but to actual incidents like the hectic anthem-singing or to
people like the paralysed old lady who could only shake her
head and say: "Triste, la guerre." They act as symbols.*

*The first passage records how the Royal Welch Fusiliers
came up in support of the Middlesex Regiment during an
attack in the Cambrun trench sector, in September, 1915:
it forms the climax to some pages of sordid horror, in which
a gas bombardment leads to appalling confusion. The second
refers to the Somme trench sector in March, 1916.*

I

WE went on up to the front line. It was full of dead and dying. The captain of the gas-company, who had kept his head and had a special oxygen respirator, had by now turned off the gas. Vermorel-sprayers had cleared out most of the gas, but we still had to wear our masks. We climbed up and crouched on the fire-step, where the gas was not so thick—gas was heavy stuff and kept low. Then Thomas arrived with the remainder of A Company and, with D, we waited for the whistle to follow the other two companies over. Fortunately at this moment the adjutant appeared. He told Thomas that he was now in command of the battalion and he didn't care a damn about orders; he was going to cut his losses. He said he would not send A and D over until he got definite orders from brigade. He had sent a runner back because telephone communication was cut, and we must wait. Meanwhile the intense bombardment that was to follow the forty minutes' discharge of gas began. It concentrated on the German front trench and wire. A good deal of it was short and we had further casualties in our trenches. The survivors of the Middlesex and of our B and C Companies in craters in No Man's Land suffered heavily.

My mouth was dry, my eyes out of focus, and my legs quaking under me. I found a water-bottle full of rum and drank about half a pint; it quieted me and my head remained clear. Samson was lying wounded about twenty yards away from the front trench. Several attempts were made to get him in. He was very badly hit and groaning. Three men were killed in these

attempts and two officers and two men wounded.
Finally his own orderly managed to crawl out to him.
Samson ordered him back, saying that he was riddled
and not worth rescuing; he sent his apologies to the
company for making such a noise. We waited for about
a couple of hours for the order to charge. The men
were silent and depressed. Sergeant Townsend was
making feeble, bitter jokes about the good old British
army muddling through and how he thanked God we
still had a navy. I shared the rest of the rum with him
and he cheered up a little. Finally a runner came with
a message that the attack was off for the present.

Rumours came down the trenches of a disaster
similar to our own in the brick-stack area, where the
Fifth Brigade had gone over, and again at Givenchy,
where it was said that men of the Sixth Brigade at the
Duck's Bill salient had fought their way into the enemy
trenches, but had been bombed out, their own supply
of bombs failing. It was said, however, that things were
better on the right, where there had been a slight wind
to take the gas over. There was a rumour that the
First, Seventh, and Forty-seventh Divisions had
broken through. My memory of that day is hazy. We
spent it getting the wounded down to the dressing-
station, spraying the trenches and dug-outs to get rid
of the gas, and clearing away the earth where trenches
were blocked. The trenches stank with a gas-blood-
lyddite-latrine smell. Late in the afternoon we watched
through our field-glasses the advance of the reserves
towards Loos and Hill 70; it looked like a real break
through. They were being heavily shelled. They were
troops of the new-army division whose staff we had

messed with the night before. Immediately to the right of us was the Highland Division, whose exploits on that day Ian Hay has celebrated in *The First Hundred Thousand*; I suppose that we were "the flat caps on the left" who "let down" his comrades-in-arms.

As soon as it was dusk we all went out to get in the wounded. Only sentries were left in the line. The first dead body I came upon was Samson's. I found that he had forced his knuckles into his mouth to stop himself crying out and attracting any more men to their death. He had been hit in seventeen places. Major Swainson, the second-in-command of the Middlesex, came crawling in from the German wire. He seemed to be wounded in the lungs, the stomach and a leg. Choate, a Middlesex second-lieutenant, appeared; he was unhurt, and together we bandaged Swainson and got him into the trench and on a stretcher. He begged me to loosen his belt; I cut it with a bowie-knife that I had bought in Béthune for use in the fighting. He said: "I'm about done for." We spent all that night getting in the wounded of the Royal Welch, the Middlesex and those of the Argyll and Sutherland who had attacked from the front trench. The Germans behaved generously. I do not remember hearing a shot fired that night, and we kept on until it was nearly dawn and we could be plainly seen; then they fired a few shots in warning and we gave it up. By this time we had got in all the wounded and most of the Royal Welch dead. I was surprised at some of the attitudes in which the dead had stiffened—in the act of bandaging friends' wounds, crawling, cutting wire. The Argyll and Sutherland had seven hundred casualties, including fourteen officers killed out of the sixteen that went over; the Middlesex five hundred and fifty casualties, including eleven officers killed.

Two other Middlesex officers besides Choate were unwounded; their names were Henry and Hill, second-lieutenants who had recently come with commissions from, I think, the Artists' Rifles; their welcome in the Middlesex had been something like mine in the Royal Welch. They had been lying out in shell-holes in the rain all day, sniping and being sniped at. Henry, according to Hill, had dragged five wounded men into his shell-hole and thrown up a sort of parapet with his hands and a bowie-knife that he was carrying. Hill had his platoon sergeant with him, screaming for hours with a stomach wound, begging for morphia; he was dying, so Hill gave him five pellets. We always carried morphia with us for emergencies like this. When Choate, Henry and Hill arrived back in the trenches with a few stragglers they reported at the Middlesex headquarters. Hill told me the story. The colonel and the adjutant were sitting down to a meat pie when he and Henry arrived. Henry said: "Come to report, sir. Ourselves and about ninety men of all companies. Mr Choate is back, unwounded, too." They looked up dully. The colonel said: "So you've come back, have you? Well, all the rest are dead. I suppose Mr Choate had better command what's left of A Company, the bombing officer will command what's left of B (the bombing officer had not gone over but remained with headquarters), Mr Henry goes to C Company, Mr Hill to D. The Royal Welch are holding the front line. We are here in support. Let me know where to find you if I want you. Good night." There was no offer to have a piece of meat pie or a drink of whisky, so they saluted and went miserably out. They were called back by the adjutant. "Mr Hill! Mr Henry!" "Sir?" Hill said that he expected a change of mind as to the propriety with which hospitality could be offered by a regular colonel and adjutant to temporary second-lieutenants in distress. But it was only to say: "Mr Hill, Mr Henry, I saw some men in the trench just now with their shoulder-straps unbuttoned and their equipment fastened anyhow. See that this practice does not occur in future. That's all." Henry heard the colonel from his bunk complaining that he had only two blankets and that it was a deucedly cold night. Choate arrived a few minutes later and reported; the others had told him of their reception. After he had saluted and reported that Major Swainson, who had been thought killed, was wounded and on the way down to the dressing-station, he leaned over the table, cut a large piece of meat pie and began eating it. This caused such surprise that nothing further was said. He finished his meat pie and drank a glass of whisky, saluted, and joined the others.

Meanwhile, I had been given command of the survivors of B Company. There were only six company officers left in the Royal Welch. Next morning there were only five. Thomas was killed by a sniper. He was despondently watching the return of the new-army troops on the right. They had been pushed blindly into the gap made by the advance of the Seventh and Forty-seventh Divisions on the previous afternoon; they did not know where they were or what they were supposed to do; their ration supply had broken down. So they flocked back, not in a panic, but stupidly, like a crowd coming back from a cup final. Shrapnel was bursting above them. We noticed that the officers were in groups of their own. We could scarcely believe our eyes, it was so odd. Thomas need not have been killed; but he was in the sort of mood in which he seemed not to care one way or the other. The Actor took command of A. We lumped our companies together after a couple of days for the sake of relieving each other on night watch and getting some sleep. The first night I agreed to take the first watch, waking him up at midnight. When I went to call him I could not wake him up; I tried everything. I shook him, shouted in his ear, poured water over him, banged his head against the side of the bed. Finally I threw him on the floor. I was desperate for want of sleep myself, but he was in a depth of sleep from which nothing could shake him, so I heaved him back on the bunk and had to finish the night out myself. Even "Stand-to!" failed to arouse him. I woke him at last at nine o'clock in the morning and he was furious with me for not having waked him at midnight.

The day after the attack we spent carrying the dead down to burial and cleaning the trench up as well as we could. That night the Middlesex held the line while the Royal Welch carried all the unbroken gas-cylinders along to a position on the left flank of the brigade, where they were to be used on the following night, September 27th. This was worse than carrying the dead; the cylinders were cast-iron and very heavy and we hated them. The men cursed and sulked, but got the carrying done. Orders came that we were to attack again. Only the officers knew; the men were only to be told just beforehand. It was difficult for me to keep up appearances with the men; I felt like screaming. It was still raining, harder than ever. We knew definitely this time that ours was only a subsidiary night attack, a diversion to help a division on our right to make the real attack. The scheme was the same as before. At four P.M. the gas was to be discharged again for forty minutes, then came a quarter of an hour's bombardment, and then the attack. I broke the news to the men about three o'clock. They took it very well. The relations of officers and men, and of senior and junior officers, had been very different in the excitement of the attack. There had been no insubordination, but a greater freedom, as if everyone was drunk together. I found myself calling the adjutant Charley on one occasion; he appeared not to mind it in the least. For the next ten days my relations with my men were like those I had with the Welsh Regiment; later discipline reasserted itself and it was only occasionally that I found them intimate.

At four P.M., then, the gas went off again. There was a strong wind and it went over well; the gas-men had brought enough spanners this time. The Germans were absolutely silent. Flares went up from the reserve lines and it seemed as though all the men in the front line were dead. The brigadier decided not to take too much for granted; after the bombardment he sent out twenty-five men and an officer of the Cameronians as a feeling-patrol. The patrol reached the German wire; there was a burst of machine-gun and rifle fire and only two wounded men regained the trench. We waited on the fire-step from four to nine o'clock, with fixed bayonets, for the order to go over. My mind was a blank except for the recurrence of "S'nice smince spie, s'nice smince spie. . . . I don't like ham, lamb or jam and I don't like roley-poley. . . ." The men laughed at my singing. The sergeant who was acting company sergeant-major said to me: "It's murder, sir." "Of course it's murder, you bloody fool," I agreed. "But there's nothing else for it, is there?" It was still raining. "But when I see's a s'nice smince spie, I asks for a helping twice. . . ." At nine o'clock we were told that the attack was put off; we were told to hold ourselves in readiness to attack at dawn.

No order came at dawn. And no more attacks were promised us after this. From the morning of September 24th to the night of October 3rd I had in all eight hours of sleep. I kept myself awake and alive by drinking about a bottle of whisky a day. I had never drank it before and have seldom drank it since; it certainly was good then. We had no blankets, greatcoats, or waterproof sheets. We had no time or material to build new shelters, and the rain continued. Every night we went out to get in the dead of the other battalions. The Germans continued to be indulgent and we had few casualties. After the first day or two the bodies swelled and stank. I vomited more than once while superintending the carrying. The ones that we could not get in from the German wire continued to swell until the wall of the stomach collapsed, either naturally or punctured by a bullet; a disgusting smell would float across. The colour of the dead faces changed from white to yellow-grey, to red, to purple, to green, to black, to slimy.

On the morning of the 27th a cry was heard from No Man's Land. It was a wounded man of the Middlesex who had recovered consciousness after two days. He was close to the German wire. Our men heard it and looked at each other. We had a lance-corporal called Baxter and he was tender-hearted. He was the man to boil up a special dixie of tea for the sentries of his section when they came off duty. When he heard the wounded man cry out he ran up and down the trench calling for a volunteer to come out with him and bring the man in. Of course no one would go; it was death to put one's head over the trench. He came running to ask me. I excused myself as the only officer in the company. I said I would come out with him at dusk, but I would not go now. So he went out himself. He jumped quickly over the parapet, then strolled across waving a handkerchief; the Germans fired at him to frighten him, but he came on, so they let him come up close. They must have heard the Middlesex man themselves. Baxter continued towards them, and, when he got up to the Middlesex man, he stopped and pointed to show the Germans what he was at. Then he dressed the man's wounds, gave him a drink of rum and some biscuits that he had with him, and told him that he would come back again for him, in the evening. He did come back for him with a stretcher-party and the man eventually recovered. I recommended Baxter for the Victoria Cross, being the only officer who had seen the thing done, but he only got a Distinguished Conduct Medal.

The Actor and I had decided to get into touch with
the battalion on our right. It was the Tenth Highland
Light Infantry. I went down their trench some time
in the morning of the 26th. I walked nearly a quarter
of a mile before seeing either a sentry or an officer.
There were dead men, sleeping men, wounded men,
gassed men, all lying anyhow. The trench had been used
as a latrine. Finally I met a Royal Engineer officer. He
said to me: "If the Boche knew what an easy job it was,
he'd just walk over and take this trench." So I came
back and told the Actor that we might expect to have
our flank in the air at any moment. We turned the
communication trench that made the boundary between the two battalions into a fire-trench facing right;
a machine-gun was mounted to put up a barrage in
case they ran. On the night of the 27th the Highlanders
mistook some of our men, who were out in No Man's
Land getting in the dead, for the enemy. They began
firing wildly. The Germans retaliated. Our men caught
the infection, but were at once told to cease fire.
"Cease fire" went along the trench until it came to the
H.L.I., who misheard it as "Retire." A panic seized
them and they came rushing back. Fortunately they
came down the trench instead of over the top. They
were stopped by a sergeant of the Fifth Scottish Rifles,
a territorial battalion now in support to ourselves and
the Middlesex. He chased them back into their trench
at the point of the bayonet.

On the 3rd of October we were relieved. The relieving troops were a composite battalion consisting of
about a hundred men of the Second Royal Warwick-
shire Regiment and about seventy Royal Welch

Fusiliers, all that was left of our own First Battalion. Hanmer Jones and Frank Jones-Bateman had both been wounded. Frank had his thigh broken with a rifle-bullet while stripping the equipment off a wounded man in No Man's Land; the cartridges in the man's pouches had been set on fire by a shot and were exploding. (He was recommended for a Victoria Cross but got nothing because no officer evidence, which is a condition of award, was available.) We went back to Sailly la Bourse for a couple of days, where the colonel rejoined us with his bandaged hand, and then further back to Annezin, a little village near Béthune, where I lodged in a two-roomed cottage with an old woman called Adelphine Heu.

II

I rejoined the First Battalion in March, finding it in the line again, on the Somme. It was the primrose season. We went in and out of the Fricourt trenches, with billets at Morlancourt, a country village at that time untouched by shell-fire. (Later it was knocked to pieces; the Australians and the Germans captured and recaptured it from each other several times, until there was nothing left except the site.) 'A' Company headquarters were in a farmhouse kitchen. We slept in our valises on the red-brick floor. The residents were an old lady and her daughter. The old lady was senile and paralysed; about all she could do was to shake her head and say: "Triste, la guerre." We called her "Triste La Guerre." Her daughter used to carry her about in her arms.

The Fricourt trenches were cut in chalk, which was better in wet weather than the La Bassée clay. We were unlucky in having a battalion-frontage where the lines came closer to each other than at any other point for miles. It was only recently that the British line had been extended down to the Somme. The French had been content, as they usually were, unless they definitely intended a battle, to be at peace with the Germans and not dig in too near. But here there was a slight ridge and neither side could afford to let the other hold the crest, so they shared it, after a prolonged dispute. It was used by both the Germans and ourselves as an experimental station for new types of bombs and grenades. The trenches were wide and tumbledown, too shallow in many places, and without sufficient traverses. The French had left relics of their nonchalance—corpses buried too near the surface; and of their love of security—a number of lousy but deep dug-outs. We busied ourselves raising the front-line parapet and building traverses to limit the damage of the trench-mortar shells that were continually falling. Every night not only the companies in the front line but both support companies were hard at work all the time. It was even worse than Cuinchy for rats; they used to run about A Company mess while we were at meals. We used to eat with revolvers beside our plates and punctuate our conversation with sudden volleys at a rat rummaging at somebody's valise or crawling along the timber support of the roof above our heads. A Company officers were gay. We had all been in our school choirs except Edmund Dadd, who sang like a crow, and we used to chant church anthems and bits of cantatas whenever things were going well. Edmund insisted on joining in.

We were at dinner one day when a Welsh boy came rushing in, hysterical with terror. He shouted out to Richardson: "Sirr, sirr, there is a trenss-mortar in my dug-out." This in sing-song Welsh made us all shout with laughter. Richardson said: "Cheer up, 33 Williams, how did a big thing like a trench-mortar happen to be in your dug-out?" But 33 Williams could not explain. He went on again and again: "Sirr, sirr, there is a trenss-mortar in my dug-out!" Edmund Dadd went out to investigate. He found that a trench-mortar shell had fallen into the trench, bounced down the dug-out steps, exploded and killed five men. 33 Williams had been lying asleep and had been protected by the body of another man; he was the only one unhit.

Our greatest trial was the canister. It was a two-gallon drum with a cylinder inside containing about two pounds of an explosive called ammonal that looked like salmon paste, smelt like marzipan, and when it went off sounded like the day of judgment. The hollow around the cylinder was filled with scrap metal apparently collected by the French villagers behind the German line—rusty nails, fragments of British and French shells, spent bullets, and the screws, nuts, and bolts that heavy lorries leave behind on the road. We dissected one canister that had not exploded and found in it, among other things, the cog-wheels of a clock and half a set of false teeth. The canister was easy to hear coming and looked harmless in the air, but its shock was as shattering as the very heaviest shell. It would blow in any but the deepest dug-outs; and the

false teeth and cog-wheels and so on would go flying
all over the place. We could not agree how a thing of
that size was fired. The problem was not solved until
1st July, when the battalion attacked from these same
trenches and found one of the canister-guns with its
crew. It was a wooden cannon buried in the earth and
fired with a time-fuse. The crew offered to surrender,
but our men refused; they had sworn for months to
get the crew of that gun.

One evening I was in the trench with Richardson
and David Thomas (near "Trafalgar Square," should
anyone remember the trench-junction) when we met
Pritchard and the adjutant. We stopped to talk.
Richardson complained what a devil of a place it was
for trench-mortars. Pritchard said: "That is where I
come in." He was the battalion trench-mortar officer
and had just been given the first two Stokes mortar-
guns that we had seen in France. Pritchard said:
"They're beauties. I've been trying them out and tomorrow I'm going to get some of my own back. I can
put four or five shells in the air at the same time."
The adjutant said: "About time, too. We've had three
hundred casualties in the last month here. It doesn't
seem so many as that because we've had no officer
casualties. In fact we've had about five hundred casualties in the ranks since Loos, and not a single officer."
Then he suddenly realized that he had said something
unlucky. David said: "Touch wood." Everybody
sprang to touch wood, but it was a French trench and
unriveted. I pulled a pencil out of my pocket; that was
wood enough for me. Richardson said: "I'm not
superstitious, anyway."

The next evening I was leading up A Company for
a working-party. B and D Companies were in the line
and we overtook C which was also going up to work.
David was bringing up the rear of C. He was looking
strange, worried about something. I had never seen
him anything but cheerful all the time I had known
him. I asked what was the matter. He said: "Oh, I'm
fed up and I've got a cold." C Company went along to
the right of the battalion frontage and we went along
to the left. It was a weird kind of night, with a bright
moon. A German occupied sap was only forty or fifty
yards away. We were left standing on the parapet
piling up the sandbags, with the moon behind us, but
the German sentries ignored us—probably because
they had work on hand themselves. It often happened
when both sides were busy putting up proper defences
that they turned a blind eye to each other's work.
Sometimes, it was said, the rival wiring-parties "as
good as borrowed each other's mallets" for hammering in the pickets. The Germans were much more
ready to live and let live than we were. (The only time,
so far as I know, besides Christmas 1914, that both
sides showed themselves in daylight without firing at
each other was once at Ypres when the trenches got so
flooded that there was nothing for it but for both sides
to crawl out on top to avoid drowning.) There was a
continual exchange of grenades and trench-mortars on
our side: the canister was going over and the men
found it difficult to get out of its way in the dark. But
for the first time we were giving the enemy as good as
they gave us. Pritchard had been using his Stokes'
mortar all day and had sent over two or three hundred

rounds; twice they had located his emplacement and
he had had to shift hurriedly.

'A' Company worked from seven in the evening
until midnight. We must have put thousands of sandbags into position, and fifty yards of front trench were
beginning to look presentable. About half-past ten
there was rifle-fire on the right and the sentries passed
down the news "officer hit." Richardson at once went
along to see who it was. He came back to say: "It's
young Thomas. He got a bullet through the neck, but
I think he's all right; it can't have hit his spine or an
artery because he's walking down to the dressing-
station." I was pleased at this news. I thought that
David would be out of it long enough perhaps to
escape the coming offensive and perhaps even the rest
of the war. At twelve o'clock we had finished for the
night. Richardson said to me: "Von Ranke" (only he
pronounced it Von Runicke—it was my regimental
nickname), "take the company down for their rum
and tea, will you? They've certainly deserved it to-
night. I'll be along in a few minutes. I'm going out
with Corporal Chamberlen to see what work the
wiring-party's been doing all this time." So I took the
men back. When we were well started I heard a couple
of shells come over somewhere behind us. I noticed
them because they were the only shells fired that night;
five-nines they seemed by the noise. We were nearly
back at Maple Redoubt, which was the name of the
support line on the reverse side of the hill, when we
heard the cry "Stretcher-bearers!" and after a while
a man came running to say: "Captain Graves is hit."
There was a general laugh and we went on; but a

stretcher-party went up anyhow to see what was wrong. It was Richardson; the shells had caught him and the corporal among the wire. The corporal had his leg blown off, and died of wounds a day or two later. Richardson had been blown into a shell-hole full of water and had lain there stunned for some minutes before the sentries heard the corporal's cries and realized what had happened. He was brought down semi-conscious; he recognized us, told us he wouldn't be long away from the company, and gave us instructions about it. The doctor said that he had no wound in any vital spot, though the skin of his left side was riddled, as we had seen, with the chalky soil blown up against him. We felt a relief in his case, as in David's, that he would be out of it for a while.

Then news came that David had died. The regimental doctor, a throat specialist in civil life, had told him at the dressing-station: "You'll be all right, only don't raise your head for a bit." David had then, it was said, taken a letter from his pocket, given it to an orderly, and said: "Post that." It was a letter written to a girl in Glamorgan, to be posted in case he got killed. Then the doctor saw that he was choking; he tried trachotomy, but it was too late. Edmund and I were talking together in the company headquarters at about one o'clock when the adjutant came in. He looked ghastly. He told us that Richardson had died at the dressing-station. His heart had been weakened by rowing (he had been in the Eight at Radley) and the explosion and the cold water had been too much for it. The adjutant said to me nervously: "You know, somehow I feel, I—I feel responsible in a way for this; what

I said yesterday at 'Trafalgar Square.' Of course, really, I don't believe in superstition, but . . ." Just at that moment there was a noise of whizz-bang shells about twenty yards off; a cry of alarm, followed by: "Stretcher bearers!" The adjutant turned quite white and we knew without being told what it meant. We hurried out. Pritchard, having fought his duel all night, and finally silenced the enemy, was coming off duty. A whizz-bang had caught him at the point where the communication trench reached Maple Redoubt; it was a direct hit. The casualties of that night were three officers and one corporal.

It seemed ridiculous when we returned without Richardson to A Company billets to find "Triste La Guerre" still alive and to hear her once more quaver out "Triste, la guerre" when her daughter explained that the *jeune capitaine* had been killed. The old woman had taken a fancy to the *jeune capitaine*; we used to chaff him about it. I felt David's death worse than any other death since I had been in France. It did not anger me as it did Siegfried. He was acting transport-officer and every night now, when he came up with the rations, he went out on patrol looking for Germans. It just made me feel empty and lost.

One of the anthems that we used to sing was: "He that shall endure to the end, shall be saved." The words repeated themselves in my head like a charm whenever things were bad. "Though thousands languish and fall beside thee, And tens of thousands around thee perish, Yet still it shall not come nigh thee." And there was another bit: "To an inheritance incorruptible. . . . Through faith unto salvation, Ready to be revealed at the last trump." For "trump" we always used to sing "crump." "The last crump" was the end of the war and would we ever hear it burst safely behind us? I wondered whether I could endure to the end with faith unto salvation. I knew that my breaking point was near now, unless something happened to stave it off. . . . It was not that I was frightened. Certainly I feared death; but I had never yet lost my head through fright, and I knew that I never would. Nor would the breakdown come as insanity; I did not have it in me. It would be a general nervous collapse, with tears and twitchings and dirtied trousers. I had seen cases like that.

From " Good-bye to All That"

" *Good-bye to All That*" *remains one of the sharpest, most honest, most memorable personal records of the first two decades of our century. The final pages of the book reveal that for the author it was necessary to write these things in order to be able to say good-bye to them at all finally. His writing makes us open-eyed and alert about the impact of such experience as the war brought, upon earlier security, and humanity, and faith. It is perhaps equally necessary that we should read them; and such phrases as " the lost generation" and " post-war disillusion" will not be so empty for us.*

By 1929, when " Good-bye to All That" was composed from earlier notes and records, Mr Graves was much admired as a subtle and original poet. There is a good selection from his poetry called " No more Ghosts" (Faber and Faber). His work in imaginative prose has also won admiration, notably the two historical novels about the emperor Claudius of Rome, " I, Claudius" and " Claudius the God." (Both have been published as Penguins. So has his own selection from his poetry.)

III

Living to Some Purpose

The Choice of a Craft
Beatrice Webb

The name of Beatrice Webb figures in "Good-bye to All That" not long after the passages chosen. For before and during and after the war there were forces at work making for life and growth, and drawing sustenance from what was finest in the life of the past. The war was catastrophic and destructive, and it precipitated a condition of moral uncertainty that is with us still. But the "affirming flame" still burned.

In 1889 had been published a book called "Fabian Essays." George Bernard Shaw had edited them, and introduced them as "a sample of the propaganda carried on by volunteer lecturers in the workmen's clubs and political associations of London." In fact they formulated the theory and practice which inspired British Socialism through the first five decades of this century. The Fabians were socialists; they were colleagues collaborating in discussion, discovery, and endeavour; they were individual thinkers who respected one another's individuality; they were advisers, not dogmatic politicians. Beatrice Webb, who married one of the most distinguished of them, herself called them "clerks to the Labour movement." With her husband, this dedicated sociologist became a decisive influence in social reconstruction and reform.

She was the daughter of a Victorian company promoter, one of a large, wealthy, and very cultured family. Chapter III of "My Apprenticeship"—indeed, the whole of that

fine classic—shows with what devotion to high purpose,
with what sympathy and understanding and resource she
set aside the comfortable, leisured and 'social' life imagined
for her, and gave herself to a vocation more worthwhile and
far more demanding: the 'craft of a social investigator.'
For her this meant not only intellectual and scientific work,
but discoveries about living and working to be made at first-
hand; a call upon tenacity, and insight into the hearts and
minds of others socially far removed from her.

"My Apprenticeship" takes the form of retrospective
narrative interspersed with quotations from diaries. In
the sequence from The Choice of a Craft that follows, ex-
cerpts from diaries are distinguished by their being inset a
little on the page; and omissions are indicated by a space.

IN the following pages I seek to describe my reaction
to the curiously compelling quality in the social
environment in which I lived; whether this was manifested in the books that I read, in the persons with
whom I associated, or in the domestic, social and political events that formed the framework of my life.
Granted intellectual curiosity, and an overpowering
impulse towards self-expression, it now seems to me
that, whatever had been my inborn gifts and defects,
the weight of circumstance would have compelled me
to investigate the history and working of social
institutions.

To win recognition as an intellectual worker was,
even before my mother's death, my secret ambition.
I longed to write a book that would be read; but I had
no notion about what I wanted to write. From my
diary entries I infer that, if I had followed my taste and

my temperament (I will not say my talent), I should
have become, not a worker in the field of sociology,
but a descriptive psychologist; either in the novel, to
which I was from time to time tempted; or (if I had
been born thirty years later) in a scientific analysis of
the mental make-up of individual men and women,
and their behaviour under particular conditions. For
there begin to appear in my diary, from 1882 onwards,
realistic scenes from country and town life, descriptions of manners and morals, analytic portraits of relations and friends—written, not with any view to self-
education, as were my abstracts, extracts and reviews,
but merely because I enjoyed writing them. It is, however, significant that these sketches from life nearly
always concern the relation of the individual to some
particular social organization: to big enterprise, or to
Parliament, to the profession of law, or of medicine or
of the Church.

The death of my mother revolutionized my life.
From being a subordinate, carrying out directions, and
having to fit into the framework of family circumstance,
studies and travels, friendships and flirtations, I became a principal, a person in authority, determining
not only my own but other people's conduct; the head
of a large household perpetually on the move; the
home, wherever located, serving as the meeting-place
of seven married sisters and their growing families; a
busy hostess in town and country, entertaining my
father's, my own and my sisters' friends. More significant than any of these routine activities was the fact
that I was my father's counsellor and my youngest

sister's virtual guardian. This position of responsibility
and authority was accentuated by my father's temperament; if he had any defect as a parent it was an over-
indulgent disposition, an over-appreciation of the
character and intelligence of those whom he loved and
those with whom he lived. And though I was not one
of the daughters who attracted his more romantic
sentiments, I was certainly one in whose judgement
and business shrewdness he had complete confidence;
a confidence due partly to my having acted, off and on,
as his private secretary and confidential attendant;
memorizing for him the various details of the unwritten "understandings" between men of affairs
which form so large a part of the machinery of big
business. I note, in passing, that apprehending, recollecting, and afterwards recording complicated series of
facts, gathered in conversation, is part of the technique
of a social investigator; and I owe the skill I had as an
interviewer to this preliminary practice with my father.
When I became the head of his household, he left it to
me to settle the why, the when and the wherefore of the
expenditure of a considerable income; indeed, he had
more than once suggested that if I "did not want to
marry" I might become his recognized associate in
business. Thus, for two or three years, I experienced
that unrestricted and unregulated use of money which
the *rentiers* term personal freedom, and the wage-
earners, who feel that they produce the commodities and
services consumed by men and women of leisure, regard as personal power. Moreover, coincident with this
increased freedom or power, perhaps arising out of it,
was a bound upward in physical and mental vigour.

From being an anaemic girl, always paying for spells of dissipation or study by periods of nervous exhaustion, often of positive illness, I became an exceptionally energetic woman, carrying on, persistently and methodically, several separate, and, in some ways, conflicting phases of life—undergoing, in fact, much of the strain and stress of a multiple personality.

Driving through the streets of London on my way from Paddington I had that curious "sensation" of power, which I suppose comes to most people who have lived within themselves, who have seldom had their self-estimation righted by competition with others. Every face in the crowded streets seemed ready to tell me its secret history if only I would watch closely enough. Again, that vain hope for a "bird's-eye view" of mankind floated before my eyes; a grasping after some spectral idea which vanished as I tried to describe its outline. My energy and my power for work were suddenly increased. I remained in a state of exaltation all the summer, possibly to some extent due to the physical effect of the high air at Murren. (General abundance of blood is a cause of emotional exaltation! H.S.) The state of "exaltation," whether moral or intellectual, must be the same, in its inherent nature, in the genius and in the ordinary person; but it is vastly different in its result. It is a spiritual isolation of yourself; a questioning of your capability of doing useful work outside the duty incumbent on an ordinary individual of the special class to which you belong.

The penalty attached to a wrong answer is greater if it err on the side of vanity. There is the probability of ridicule, and what is worse infinitely, the certainty of comparative uselessness. Cynicism, too, helps humility to conquer in this crisis. It is so very doubtful whether works (either of thought or of action) of the moderately gifted man have any permanent effect. If he is representative, he is a mere instrument, and many as good ones lie to hand. If he resist the stream, he is powerless to divert the fearful current of human tendency. My little dream was broken by the friendly shake of kindly persons who caught me napping and neglecting work in which they were interested. Mathematics, too, effectually sobered me. It is a good foot-measure of ability which can be used in private. On the whole, the new year begins with a determination to devote myself first of all to practical life; if there is energy to spare, "surely I can do what I like with mine own!"

It would be amusing to make studies of human beings, with the same care I bestowed on imitating bits of rock, stick and root. The six months spent on drawing, though wasted as far as accomplishment goes, certainly increased sensitiveness to colour and form. I remember, that winter, what keen delight the curve of a tree branch, the gradation of colour in a carrot or turnip, gave me. The vilest things in Nature had an interest and even a beauty of their own. And, since my life will be much spent in society, an attempt to describe the men and women I meet will add interest to it, and give me a more delicate appreciation of their characteristics.

In most of us there is a desire to express our thoughts, feelings or impressions. Women generally choose music or drawing, but there is really no more pretension in writing, so long as one does not humbug oneself as to the value of the stuff written. And there is this advantage, that language is the ordinary medium for influence in practical life; and that, even if we ignore the great advantage of writing in its development of thought, clearness and plausibility of expression are good allied to the more important qualities of character and mind. Morley says we moderns limit our ideas of redeeming the time to the two pursuits of reading books and making money; and, roughly speaking, the number of books read and digested during this past year is equivalent in one's own estimation to work done!

It is a difficult question whether the present "intellectualism" is overestimated in its good effects. Just at present, I fancy there is a reaction against the idea that intellectual education is the cure for all evils. Certainly, the persons who are universally interested and universally useless make up rather a dreary society. Does culture increase power to act? I am inclined to think it increases the power but decreases the desire.

The first point to be settled was how to reconcile the rival pulls on time and energy, on the one hand, of family affection, backed up by the Victorian code of feminine domesticity; and, on the other, of a domineering curiosity into the nature of things, reinforced by an awakening desire for creative thought and literary expression. Some claims were beyond doubt. To be my father's companion in business and travel was not merely a continuous delight but also a liberal education. Personal sympathy as well as a sense of duty was roused by my little sister's chronic ill-health. But there were other assumptions with regard to the whole duty of woman that I refused to accept. According to the current code, the entire time and energy of an un-married daughter—especially if she was the responsible mistress of the home—were assumed to be spent, either in serving the family group, or in entertaining and being entertained by the social circle to which she belonged. There was, it is true, a recognized counter-claim, the right to end this apprenticeship by accom-plishing her masterpiece, making a "good marriage," by which she would graduate into the goodly company of prosperous matrons, thus adding to the corporate influence of the family. A code implies a court to inter-pret it. In my case, the solid phalanx of seven married sisters, with the seven brothers-in-law in reserve as assessors, proved to be, I gladly admit it, a tolerant and kindly jury of inquiry and presentment. But, like other potential law-breakers, I was determined to evade, or at any rate to limit, the court's jurisdiction. In so far as the health and happiness of father and sister were con-cerned, or the disposal of the family income, I fully recognized the right of the family jury to intervene. But I silently withdrew all my own aspirations and plans for self-culture and self-expression from family discussion—a reserve which entailed isolation and lone-liness.

.   .   .   .   .

Alongside of this inward conflict is a recognition that (probably owing to this egotism) I am losing ground in the affections of my sisters. Of course there will be unavoidable criticism, and some of it will be unjustified. It is no use being over-sensitive —but if one wishes to feel philosophically towards it, one must be honestly convinced of the rightness and thoroughness of one's own intentions.

The following entries in my diary, during the first year of my newly found position of an independent hostess in London society, reveal the strain and stress of this internal struggle between the desire for self-development and self-expression and the more conventional calls of family duty, reinforced by the promptings of personal vanity and social ambition.

Shall I give myself up to society and make it my aim to succeed therein; or shall I only do so as far as duty calls me, keeping my private life much as it has been for the last nine months? On the whole the balance is in favour of society. It is going with the stream, and pleasing my people. It is doing a thing thoroughly that I must do partially. It is taking opportunities instead of making them. It is risking less, and walking on a well-beaten track in pleasant company. The destination is not far distant; no unusual amount of power is wanted to arrive there; and lastly, and perhaps this is the reason which weighs most with me, there is less presumption in the choice.

Therefore, I solemnly dedicate my energies for the next five months to the cultivation of the social instincts—trusting that the good daemon within me will keep me from all vulgarity of mind, insincerity and falseness. I would like to go amongst men and women with a determination to know them; to humbly observe and consider their characteristics; always remembering how much there is in the most inferior individual which is outside and beyond one's understanding. Every fresh intimacy strengthens the conviction of one's own powerlessness to comprehend fully any other nature, even when one watches it with love. And without sympathy there is an impassable barrier to the real knowledge of the inner workings which guide the outer actions of human beings. Sympathy, or rather *accepted* sympathy, is the only instrument for the dissection of character. All great knowers and describers of human nature must have possessed this instrument. The perfection of the instrument depends no doubt on a purely intellectual quality, analytical imagination—this, again, originating in subjective complexity of motive and thought. But unless this latter quality is possessed to an extraordinary degree, insight into other natures is impossible, unless we subordinate our interest in self and its workings to a greater desire to understand others. Therefore the resolution which has been growing in my mind is, that I will fight against my natural love of impressing others, and prepare my mind to receive impressions. And as fast as I receive impressions I will formulate them, thereby avoiding the general haziness of

out line which follows a period of receptivity
without an attempt of expression.

A pleasant bedroom in front of the house and
looking towards the west (I write when we are
settled in Prince's Gate for the London season). In
the afternoon I can sit here and watch the sun slowly
setting behind the Museum buildings and gardens
. . . undisturbed by the rushing life of the great city;
only the brisk trottings and even rollings of the well-
fed horses and well-cushioned carriages. Altogether,
we are in the land of luxury; we are living in an
atmosphere of ease, satiety and boredom, with prospect and retrospect of gratified and mortified vanity.
Father has found occupation in enquiring into, and
to some extent organizing, a large railway amalgama-
tion scheme: the promoters anxious to get his time,
and still more his name. Secretary Price called this
afternoon. Cleverly managed to insinuate the "we"
into it. Father really anxious for work. Still suffers
silent agony and lonely grief for mother; his sorrow
is permanent though intermittent. There is a deep
sadness in decaying power, more terrible to me than
death itself. And all who have passed the prime of
life, who have lived those few golden years for work,
must exhibit this decline in the power for *persistent*
work. I do not wonder that men should turn from
human nature to study, with absorbing interest, life
in the lower forms. There is so much that is terrible
and awful in mental organization, lit up as it is by
one's own self-consciousness, and surrounded by
that dark background of annihilation. Constantly

as I walk in one of the crowded streets of London, and watch the faces of the men and women who push past me, lined, furrowed, and sometimes contorted by work, struggle and passion, and think that all this desire and pain, this manifold feeling and thought are but a condition of force and matter, phantom-like forms built up to be destroyed, a hopelessness overtakes me, paralysing all power of wishing and doing. Then I sink into inertia, relieved only by a languid curiosity as to the variations in structure and function of those individuals who will let me observe them and enquire of them. Cold-blooded enquiry takes the place of heartfelt sympathy. But this one should shake off sternly. . . .

Now my life is divided sharply into the thoughtful part and the active part (I note a month later), completely unconnected one with the other. They are, in fact, an attempt to realize the different and almost conflicting ideals, necessitating a compromise as to energy and time which has to be perpetually readjusted. My only hope is that the ideal one is hidden from the world, the truth being, that in my heart of hearts I'm ashamed of it and yet *it is* actually the dominant internal power. Fortunately for me, all external forces support the other motive, so perhaps the balance is a pretty just one. But it is a curious experience moving about among men and women, talking much, as you are obliged to do, and never mentioning those thoughts and problems which are your *real life*, and which absorb, in their pursuit and solution, all the earnestness of your nature. This doubleness of motive, still more this dissemblance towards the world you live in, extending even to your own family, must bring with it a feeling of unreality; worse, a loss of energy in the sudden transitions from the one life to the other. Happily, one thing is clear to me—the state of doubtfulness will not be of long duration; and the work that is done during that state will not be useless to me whichever vocation my nature and my circumstances eventually force me into. I shall surely some day have the veil withdrawn and be allowed to gaze unblinded on the narrow limits of my own possibilities.

In this whirl of town society life (I sum up towards the end of the season of 1883) the superficial part of my small intellect and the animal part of my nature are alike stimulated. My aim in life, the motives which have moved me in the best times of the past are blurred and misty. All now is uncertain. I wander h ther and thither in search after gratification, gradually exhausting the credit account of "good motive"; the small experience I pick up being saturated by an ever-increasing perplexity at the queerness of things. Possibly, in our mental life, when we are not forced into a groove of activity, we have periods of effort and periods of receptivity, during which latter state we collect the materials we afterwards form into action; into a governing motive. Anyhow, though, on the whole, life in this phase is pleasurable, there still remains lurking in the depths of one's nature a profound discontent; a doubt as to the usefulness of this careless noting of things, and a contempt for one's own nature in its enjoyment of these petty gratifications, and a somewhat unpleasant surprise at the presence of feelings hitherto ignored or quietly passed over as transient and unimportant.

This is the last word in my diary about what used to be called, in the reign of Queen Victoria, "Society," with a big S. The picture stored in my memory of that unpleasing social entity, a state of mind and form of activity, on the part of the upper ten thousand, which, I am told by those who ought to know, was finally killed by the Great War, has been set forth in the first chapter of this book. Here I recall that the special characteristic which most distressed me, during the two years I acted as hostess in my father's London and country homes, was the cynical effrontery with which that particular crowd courted those who possessed, or were assumed to possess, personal power; and the cold swiftness with which the same individuals turned away from former favourites when these men or women had passed out of the limelight. Moreover, it was clear that personal vanity, with its humiliating ups and downs of inflation and depression, and with its still meaner falsification, was an "occupational disease" of entertaining and being entertained; and, realizing my own constitutional weakness in this direction, flight from temptation seemed the better part of valour. But dissatisfaction with my own and other people's human nature was not the only, not perhaps the main reason for my gradual withdrawal from social functions throughout 1884 and 1885, in order to spend my free time as a rent-collector in the East End of London. What happened was that the time-spirit had, at last, seized me and compelled me to concentrate all my free energy in getting the training and the raw material for applied sociology; that is, for research into the constitution and working of social organization, with a view to bettering the life and labour of the people.

Looking back from the standpoint of today (1926), it seems to me that two outstanding tenets, some would say, two idols of the mind, were united in this mid-Victorian trend of thought and feeling. There was the current belief in the scientific method, in that intellectual synthesis of observation and experiment, hypothesis and verification, by means of which alone all mundane problems were to be solved. And added to this belief in science was the consciousness of a new motive; the transference of the emotion of self-sacrificing service from God to man.

In these latter days of deep disillusionment, now that we have learnt, by the bitter experience of the Great War, to what vile uses the methods and results of science may be put, when these are inspired and directed by brutal instinct and base motive, it is hard to understand the naïve belief of the most original and vigorous minds of the 'seventies and 'eighties that it was by science, and by science alone, that all human misery would be ultimately swept away. This almost fanatical faith was perhaps partly due to hero-worship. For who will deny that the men of science were the leading British intellectuals of that period; that it was they who stood out as men of genius with international reputations; that it was they who were the self-confident militants of the period; that it was they who were routing the theologians, confounding the mystics, imposing their theories on philosophers, their inventions on capitalists, and their discoveries on medical men; whilst they were at the same time snubbing the artists, ignoring the poets and even casting doubts on the capacity of the politicians?

However stimulating and enlightening may be social intercourse with men of mark, their casual conversations at London dinner-parties or during country-house visits cannot take the place of disciplined experiments and observation under expert direction in University laboratories or hospital wards. Any such training, even where open to women, was flagrantly out of bounds for a woman who had my extensive and complicated home duties. Hence the pitifully ineffectual attempts, recorded in my diary, to educate myself, first in algebra and geometry, described in the opening of this chapter as ending in nothing more substantial than a ghost; and secondly in the following London season, in the intervals of home-keeping for my father and little sister, and of entertaining and being entertained, in physiology, partly under the direction of a woman science-teacher, and partly by casual attendance on my brother-in-law, William Harrison Cripps, the well-known surgeon, while he was making his microscopic examination into cancer.

The first morning's work with Willie Cripps preparing specimens (here follows an elaborate description of technique of microscopic work); read through W.H.C.'s *Adenoid Diseases of the Rectum*; had great difficulty in understanding owing to technical phraseology and my ignorance of the subject-matter which he discusses. In my physiological studies must keep clear and distinct two lines of enquiry (1) how a particular organic substance became as it now is, (2) and what is at present its actual structure. Surely, a full knowledge of the present structure should precede the study of "becoming"; unless one was able to see every stage of the evolution.

Enjoy sitting in that cool room, with fresh breeze through, and green trees on both sides, in an out-of-the-way corner of London (I write about one of the lessons with the science-teacher). Before us on the table, diagrams, microscopic sections, and various dissections—these last do not distress me but give me a genuine pleasure to pick to pieces. One leaves behind all personalities, and strives hard to ascertain the constitution of things, a constitution which to us is eternal and dependent on no one manifestation of it. To me there is a deep and perplexing pathos in this study of life and death, which to some natures might become almost tragic, while in others it develops that half-sad, half-enjoyable, spectator's interest, pleasant in so far as it removes us far above the petty struggles of mean motive and conflicting interest, and sad in as much as it withdraws from our affections their permanency and from our aspirations their motive. In me, such a study strengthens necessarianism; and as I hurry down Tottenham Court Road, and jostle up against men and women of the people, with their various expressions of determined struggle, weak self-indulgence, and discontented effort, the conviction that the fate of each individual is governed by conditions born of the "distant past" is irresistibly forced upon me.

"Referring to your microscopic work," writes my guide, philosopher and friend in the following autumn, "I wish you would take up some line of enquiry, say such an one as the absorbent organs in the leaves, roots and seeds of plants (you will find an indication of them at the end of the *Biology*, but nobody has worked at them to any extent). Great zest is given to work when you have a definite end in view and it becomes both an interest and a discipline. By Xmas I hope you will have something to show me."

But in spite of this injunction, and although I realized the value of physical science as a training in scientific method, the whole subject-matter of natural science bored me. I was not interested in rocks and plants, grubs and animals, not even in man considered merely as a biped, with the organs of a biped. What roused and absorbed my curiosity were men and women, regarded—if I may use an old-fashioned word —as "souls," their past and present conditions of life, their thoughts and feelings and their constantly changing behaviour. This field of inquiry was not, as yet, recognized in the laboratories of the universities, or in other disciplined explorations of the varieties of human experience. I may add, by the way, that what turned me away from psychology, even the "psychology" to be found in books, was what seemed to me the barren

futility of the textbooks then current. Instead of the
exact description of the actual facts of individual minds,
reacting to particular environments and developing in
various directions, I seemed to find nothing but arbit-
rary definitions of mind in the abstract, which did not
correspond with the mental life of any one person, and
were in fact nothing but hypothetical abstractions from
an idealized reflection of the working of the author's
own mind—that is, of a superior person of a highly
developed race—an idealization which apparently led
to an ungrounded belief in the universal prevalence,
throughout human society, of that rare synthetic gift,
enlightened self-respect! I am afraid that, in my haste,
I regarded the manipulation of these psychological
abstractions as yielding no more accurate information
about the world around me than did the syllogisms of
formal logic. For any detailed description of the complexity of human nature, of the variety and mixture in
human motive, of the insurgence of instinct in the garb
of reason, of the multifarious play of the social environment on the individual ego and of the individual ego
on the social environment, I had to turn to novelists
and poets, to Fielding and Flaubert, to Balzac and
Browning, to Thackeray and Goethe. In all this range
of truth-telling fiction the verification of the facts or of
the conclusions drawn from the facts was impractic-
able. If I have any vain regrets for absent opportunities
it is exactly this: that I grew up to maturity as a socio-
logical investigator without a spell of observation and
experiment in the modern science of psychology.

Thrown back on books, books, and again, books, I
began to select these, not in order to satisfy curiosity

and extend interest in life, but deliberately so as to forge an instrument of discovery about human nature in society.

But the scientific method of reasoning, so it seemed to my practical mind, was not an end in itself; it was the means by which a given end could be pursued. It did not, and as I thought could not, yield the purpose of life. What it did was to show the way, and the only way, in which the chosen purpose could be fulfilled. To what end, for what purpose, and therefore *upon what subject-matter* was the new faculty of the intellect to be exercised? And here I come to the second element of the mid-Victorian Time-Spirit: the emotion, which like the warp before the woof, gives strength and direction to the activities of the intellect. I suggest it was during the middle decades of the nineteenth century that, in England, the impulse of self-subordinating service was transferred, consciously and overtly, from God to man. It would be interesting to trace the first beginnings of this elusive change of feeling. How far was it latent in the dogma that underlay the rise of American Democracy, that all men are born free and equal, with equal rights to life, liberty and the pursuit of happiness? I recall the saying of a well-known leader of the American ethical movement: "As a free-born citizen, I deny the existence of an autocratic Supreme Being to whom I, and all other men, owe obedience and worship; it offends my American sense of independence and equality!" How far was the passing of the Kingdom of God and the coming of the Kingdom of Man implicit in the "Liberty, Equality, and Fraternity" of the French Revolution, with its worship of the Goddess of Reason? We certainly find this new version of "the whole duty of man" in the characteristic political maxim of the British Utilitarians, which prescribed, as the object of human effort, the greatest happiness of the greatest number. With a more romantic content we see it in the life and work of Robert Owen, with his "worship of the supremely good principle in human nature," which became a "social bible," promulgated by "social missionaries" in a "social cathedral."

In the particular social and intellectual environment in which I lived, this stream of tendencies culminated in Auguste Comte's union of the "religion of humanity" with a glorification of science, in opposition to both theology and metaphysics, as the final stage in the development of the human intellect. And once again I note that the reading of books was in my case directed and supplemented by friendly intercourse with the men and women most concerned with the subject-matter of the books. As a student I was familiar with the writings of the most famous of the English disciples and admirers of Auguste Comte. I had learnt my lesson from George Henry Lewes. I delighted in John Stuart Mill's *Autobiography*, and had given to his *System of Logic* and *Principles of Political Economy* an assiduous though somewhat strained attention. Above all, the novels of George Eliot had been eagerly read and discussed in the family circle.

The result is memorized in a scene on the Westmorland moors in the autumn of 1879, two or three years before my mother's death.

Two girls, aged twenty-five and twenty-one respectively, stride across the Rusland bog towards the Old Man of Coniston, in a driving mist, with packets of sandwiches and cases of cigarettes bulging out of short and shabby waterproofs. They are discussing vigorously their readings from Auguste Comte. In these discussions the elder one, Margaret, always takes the leading part, as she reads six hours to the younger girl's two. The three stages in the development of the human intellect are accepted without demur; "Though how does this fit in with Buckle's climatic and increased productivity theory?" reflects Beatrice, conscious of having just completed a painstaking review of Buckle's *History of Civilization* in her private MS. book—secret writing which not even her one pal among her sisters is invited to read. Presently they come to rest on a dripping stone wall. After vainly attempting to light a cigarette, Margaret, with genial smile, glittering black eyes and long wisps of lank brown hair flying in the winds, sums up her criticism.

"Dreadful old pedant; horrid French; what a dark chasm in style between him and Voltaire. Some of his ideas detestable; others absurd. That spiritual power, I hate it. Having kicked religion out of the front door of the human intellect, why should it sneak in through the servants' hall? For after all, Beatrice," with rising acerbity, "all Comte's humans are servile. The man worships the woman. Who wants to worship any one, leave alone a woman? And the woman turns out, in the end, to be no better than a domestic servant with no life of her own. Thank heavens, he puts the working man in his right place; Great Hearts, may be; we've all got to think of them in order to do them good. But they've just got to obey; no more strikes; jolly good thing too!"

Short pause while Beatrice, having lit her cigarette by manipulating the match-box (a trick taught her sitting out with a ballroom partner in a country-house garden in the early hours of a July morning), hands the stump to Margaret, who lights up and continues in a more complacent tone.

"Rather like that notion of a committee of bankers to rule the world. The Barclays, Buxtons, and Hoares strike me as a solid lot; dull but solid; just the sort father likes us to marry, and one likes one's sisters to marry."

"But why a committee of *bankers*?" interposes the younger one. "Why not chairmen of railway companies, shipowners—for that matter, timber merchants? Machinery, raw material, trade routes, what do bankers know about them? And whether you like it or not, there's the working class who've got votes and mean to have more."

Margaret, with a note of good-tempered contempt —"My dear child, working men just don't count; it's money that counts, and the bankers have got it. Not brains, but money." And with a rising crescendo of conviction—"Credit; credit, Beatrice; it is *credit* that rules the world. Men and women have just got to follow the bankers' loans, or clear out. Over and again I have watched it. Remember how Baring and Glyn beat father about that new railway in Canada, which after all didn't pay. Father had the brains but they had the money; and it was *he* who had to resign, not they."

Long pause: Beatrice doubts the sister's synonymous use of the terms "money" and "credit." "Father said," she muses, "that the amount of credit depended on the state of mind of the capitalist: a state of mind which does not always correspond with the state of affairs; hence trade booms and depressions. Money was a commodity like any other commodity, except that it had a specialized use and a legalized status. 'My little Bee,' he added, with his dear beaming smile, 'might think out for herself whether cheques are money or credit and let me know.' And I never did so," she ruefully recollects.

Margaret, having swung round and jumped off the wall on the other side—"Come along, Beatrice, we've got to get up there before we eat our lunch; I'm getting hungry. . . . The plain truth is that all this fantastic stuff about the future is nonsense. No one knows or can know what is going to happen to the world. The root question raised by Comte—the only one that concerns you and me, is whether we are all of us, here and now, to tumble over each other and get in each other's way by trying to better the world, or whether we are each one of us to pursue his or her own interest according to common sense. I'm for each one of us looking after our own affairs. Of course I include family affairs. One has to look after father and mother, husband and children, brothers and sisters. But there it stops. Perhaps," slowly and doubtfully, "if there is time and money to spare, sisters' children." Briskly dogmatic—

"Certainly not uncles or aunts; still less, cousins; they're not as good as business associates, and only a shade better than London acquaintances. As for the service of man, the religion of humanity; Heavens, Beatrice, what *does* it mean? It is just underbred theology, with no bishops to bless it."

So spake the Ego that denies. Some forty years afterwards, roused by a mother's sorrow for one son dead on the battlefield, another in a prison cell on grounds of conscience, the Ego that affirms impels her to stand fast by the brotherhood of man, whether friend or enemy; and in particular to sacrifice fast-failing strength to prison reform, where she builded better than the world knows. (*In the autumn of 1880 Margaret married Henry Hobhouse, of Hadspen, Somersetshire. She had seven children—her youngest son being killed in the War. She died in 1920, her husband and five children surviving her. In the last years of her life, owing to the imprisonment during the War of her eldest child Stephen (who had joined the Society of Friends, and had refused to be burdened with property or the prospect of property) as an "absolutist" conscientious objector, she published "An Appeal to Cæsar," and became interested in prison reform, initiating the inquiry which eventuated in the remarkable report by Stephen Hobhouse and Fenner Brockway, entitled "English Prisons To-day," 1922. Many of the proposals of this report have been embodied in the recent transformation of prison administration in England, effected, not by Act of Parliament, but as a result of the silent conversion of the Home Office bureaucracy.*)

Social questions are the vital questions of to-day: they take the place of religion. I do not pretend to solve them. Their solution seems largely a matter of temperament. Still, the most insignificant mind has a certain bias, has an intellectual as well as a moral conscience. If we wilfully defy the laws of our special mental constitution we must suffer the penalty of a diseased and twisted nature, and must leave life conscious of faithlessness to the faith that is in us. . . . A higher standard of motive is asked for in social action than in any other. . . . The social reformer professes to be an uncompromising idealist; he solemnly declares that he is working for the public weal. His whole authority, derived from public opinion, arises from the faith of the people in his honesty of purpose and strength of understanding. If he uses his mind to manipulate facts, and twist them so that they shall serve his own personal interests, if the craving for power is greater than the desire for truth, he is a traitor to the society towards which he professes loyal service.

Now, without pretending to sum up the influence of the time-spirit on the social activities of the last quarter of the nineteenth century, what is clear is that upon me—in 1883, a woman of twenty-five—it led to a definite conclusion. From the flight of emotion away from the service of God to the service of man, and from the current faith in the scientific method, I drew the inference that the most hopeful form of social service was the craft of a social investigator. And some such conclusion seems to have been reached by many of my contemporaries. For detailed descriptions of the life and labour of the people in all its various aspects, sensational or scientific, derived from personal observation or statistical calculation, become a characteristic feature of the publications of this period, whether newspapers or magazines, plays or novels, the reports of philanthropic organizations or the proceedings of learned societies. It may be said that this novel concentration of attention on the social condition of the people was due neither to intellectual curiosity nor to the spirit of philanthropy, but rather to a panic fear of the newly enfranchised democracy. But this is looking at the same fact from another standpoint. For even the most fanatical Socialist asserted that his hopes for the future depended on a deliberately scientific organization of society, combined with the growth among the whole body of the people of the desire and capacity for disinterested social service.

It was in the autumn of 1883 that I took the first step as a social investigator, though I am afraid the adventure was more a sentimental journey than a scientific exploration. What had been borne into me during my book studies was my utter ignorance of the manual-working class, that is, of four-fifths of my fellow-countrymen. During the preceding London season I had joined a Charity Organization Committee and acted as one of its visitors in the slums of Soho; but it was clear to me that these cases of extreme destitution, often distorted by drink and vice, could no more be regarded as a fair sample of the wage-earning class than the "sporting set" of London society could be considered representative, either in conduct or in intelligence, of the landed aristocracy and business and professional class, out of which its individual members had usually sprung. How was I to get an opportunity of watching day by day, in their homes and in their work-shops, a sufficient number of normal manual working families to enable me to visualize the class as a whole; to understand what was meant by chronic poverty and insecurity of livelihood; to ascertain whether such con-ditions actually existed in any but a small fraction of the great body of the people? Were the manual workers what I was accustomed to call civilized? What were their aspirations, what was their degree of education, what their capacity for self-government? How had this class, without administrative training or literary cul-ture, managed to initiate and maintain the network of Nonconformist chapels, the far-flung friendly societies, the much-abused Trade Unions, and that queer type of shop, the Co-operative store?

From " My Apprenticeship"

There follows the matchless account of the visit to Bacup, the East Lancashire manufacturing town, which gave her the opportunity of discovery she had waited for. This is the prose of the private journal and of informal retrospect: prose that comes directly from the tensions of daily living. It is literature by accident, the accident of dedicated char-acter and strong insight. The prose registers Beatrice Webb's underlying capacity and her driving power. It was not only intellectual or scientific aptitude or a bent of the will. It was imagination, it was the finest kind of respect for other people, it was a triumph of tact. Notice the quick, subtle appraisements of people and motives—and of herself. Notice, too, references and hints (like the touches of George Eliot in the prose, the admiration for that great novelist, the affection for Herbert Spencer) that show her drawing upon the finest qualities of her own social background, even while she gives a penetrating report upon that background.

　"My Apprenticeship" has been published as a Pelican book. "Our Partnership" followed; and two more volumes drawn from her fascinating diaries of public and private life have appeared since her death in 1943. The first remains the most important. There are not many books comparable with it. One in particular suggests itself as worth taking up, however—especially if the later journals of Beatrice Webb give pleasure and deep interest: Sir Ronald Storr's "Orientations" (Nicholson and Watson). Here too is the personal record of a distinguished public figure, given in a slightly more formal (and far less vital) prose, and revealing a comprehension, a sympathetic tact, out of the ordinary.

Guiding to a Goal
E. M. Forster

E. M. Forster's biography of the Cambridge scholar, teacher, and writer, Goldsworthy Lowes Dickinson, tries to convey the feel of a fine personality. This excerpt deals with his faith and practice as a teacher; it takes us to the centre of his vitality. And Mr Forster suffuses his apparently casual and easy prose with an affectionate respect for the way of life that Dickinson here symbolizes.

Dickinson, a Fellow and Lecturer of King's College, was one of a group of Cambridge philosophers, historians, and economists who established an important influence during the first decades of this century. Dickinson himself (as Mr Forster here shows) connected the group with the Fabians, and the London School of Economics. Others were to connect it more lastingly but less usefully with the world of Bloomsbury; and Bloomsbury has played, and still plays, a significant part in modern cultural life. In Dickinson belief in the free play of intelligence, in the value of scholarship, and in the value of personal relationships, goes side by side with a clear sense of moral and social responsibility; and the kind of man he was, is more important than anything he accomplished in the public world; for his books are useful but not great, and only his tireless advocacy of the League of Nations can be said to have made even a small mark outside the university world. But for himself—let Mr Forster introduce what is to follow: " He was beloved, affectionate,

*unselfish, witty, charming . . . he did not merely increase our
experience: he left us more alert for what has not yet been
experienced, and more hopeful about other men, because he
had lived."*

THIS chapter covers events between the renewal of
his fellowship and the outbreak of the war, with
the exception of his visits to America and the East and
their implications, which will be considered separately.
The outstanding event is his emergence as a teacher.
He becomes more and more anxious to stimulate, and
less interested in learning and artistic expression for
their own sakes. His studies, his political opinions, his
lecturing, his published works, his capacity for friendship, his interest in the young—all flow into a single
channel, which might be called educational if the word
were not so misused, and "maieutic" if the word were
not a little pedantic. Though he does not remind one
of Socrates personally, though he had neither the nagging qualities which wore down the sophists, nor the
physical high spirits, nor the toughness to fight at
Potidaea, nor the desire to fight there, yet Socrates is
his master. It is as a teacher who was constantly being
taught that he must be regarded during these twenty-
one years.

A letter to May, dating from the threshold of this
period, will serve as an informal preface to it, as did the
letter to Grant in the case of the period preceding.
While quoting in full I have missed out most of the
underlinings, because like the stresses in his talk they
are faint, the pen travelling lightly beneath the word,
and only emphasizing half of it.

KING'S COLLEGE, CAMBRIDGE
March 10th, 1889

Writing the date reminds me of your birthday, for which I send all possible good wishes and greetings—and would send a present if I had one! Isn't this spring weather delicious? At least it is here—snowdrops and crocuses and aconite everywhere, and that delicious sense of beginning, which is so much better than fruition.

'And then, and then came spring and rose in hand.
My threadbare garment of repentance tore,'

which is a sentiment of Omar Khayyam I quite understand. Fred was here last Sunday, that perhaps was partly why I didn't write, and also I was busy with papers. I'm not pleased with my lectures, but I don't quite know how they ought to be; they're certainly not interesting enough, and I should be very angry with myself if I were in the audience.

I'm growing magnificent ideas of what a university *ought* to be; it ought to lead thought, as it did in the Reformation, and not skulk behind and talk of vested rights. And there never were places with such chances as Oxford and Cambridge. I don't want them popularised, I want them to educate leaders, and let there be other universities to educate the rest. So we ought to teach politics somehow through history, which has always been O.B.'s idea, and like all his ideas is good. We do teach people how to live, how to make friendship, etc, but I don't think we teach them, as a rule, how to think—*i.e.*, how to apply their knowledge to here and now. All this is 'ideal,' and one gets ashamed of what's ideal, but it may become practical. I shall probably come to London next Thursday week, or thereabouts. The Choral Symphony must have been fine. We had Mozart's

Requiem on Thursday in chapel; music, different to anything else of his. Great as Beethoven, I think. Best love. I heard of you from Miss Johnson. Isn't she nice? A. Berry was up yesterday, and Lennie—(?) gets nicer and nicer.

Lennie's surname is indecipherable, but that he got nicer and nicer there is little doubt: most of the people who constantly saw Goldie did that, though he did not realize why.

He ceased to be a bad lecturer and became a good one as soon as he ceased to "lecture" and began to speculate aloud. In his University Extension days he had tried to convey facts, to impose opinions and to arouse emotions, but he modified considerably on all these three points. As for facts, he soon realized that they are best learned from text-books and that the lecturer who ladles them out to an audience who gobbles them down is only carrying on the educational traditions of the Misses Woodman's morning classes for the sons of gentlemen. As for opinions: the formation of these was indeed his chief aim, but his method became more tentative as his grasp on reality tightened. He believed that his own opinions were right or he would not have held them, but he never dictated them or desired that they should be accepted; instead, he encouraged clear thinking and decent feeling and hoped that on such a soil right opinions would flourish. And as for arousing emotion: he neither aimed at this nor did he achieve it in any crude sense. The seriousness of the theme provided its own emotion. Knowledge of the past will help us to control the future, and unless we can control the future our happiness, private and public, is at the mercy of chance. Thus a subject like the History of Political Theory which is on the face of it academic, became arresting and disquieting under his treatment, because he made his audience feel they might influence Fate. For instance the dilemma of Jeremy Bentham—how can a selfish statesman provide an unselfish policy?—appeared as real to his audience as it had been when Bentham formulated it.

Dickinson had the external framework necessary for a lecturer; he was accurate, well informed, polite, dignified, clear, punctual. But it was the light within which impressed his audiences—no will-of-the-wisp of the Coleridge variety, but a light which for all its spontaneity shone steadily and guided to a goal. His voice and his expression are not easily conveyed, because they were not dramatic; it was no mission of his to vibrate with emotion, or to point out the choice before us with his forefinger, or to stamp upon international anarchy with his foot. He left such achievements to orators. What did come across was a modulation in the tones and a light upon the face, which showed that the whole man was alive and was working at a distance to bring help. This helpfulness was present at all times, but it was unusually moving when it shone through the formality of a lecture-framework.

His official subject at King's was Political Science, then locally known by the title of Analytical and Deductive Politics, and he continued in it two terms a year from his appointment in 1896 to 1920, when he resigned the lectureship. He was, during precisely the same period, lecturing at the London School of

Economics, and some reference must now be made to his activity there. It has not the glamour of the Cambridge connection, and it is not so generally known, but it was important to his audiences and to himself.

The London School of Economics and Political Science was founded in 1895, chiefly owing to the efforts of the Sidney Webbs. Dickinson's early socialism had brought him into contact with Fabianism, and he had already arranged for visits to Cambridge from Webb, Hubert Bland, Olivier, Bernard Shaw, and others then belonging to the group. The visits had caused some excitement. Webb had argued with McTaggart, neither side scoring a victory. Bland had talked football to the young men. Shaw had lectured brilliantly, also telling a story about an Irish uncle who thought he was in heaven and hung from the ceiling in a basket dressed in gauze. Asked on behalf of Dr Westcott what his moral basis was, Shaw had replied to Dickinson on a postcard, "Ask the old boy what his is, and tell him mine's the same." So, though Dickinson's temperament was far from Fabian and his methods anything but statistical, it was natural that he should be invited to teach at the newly established School. His connection began in 1896. In 1911 he was put on the permanent staff as lecturer in Political Science; in 1920 he resigned. His lectures at the School were, so far as their subjects and general outlook went, a repetition of the courses delivered at Cambridge. Here is a complete list. He began with "The Machinery of Administration in England." He followed this by courses on "The Use of Political Terms," "The Bases of Political Obligation," "The Structure of the Modern

State," "Popular Government," "The British Empire and other Composite States," "Some Theories of the Basis of Political Obligation," "The Government of the British Empire," "The Structure of the Modern State," "The Functions of the Modern State," "The Central Government of England comparatively treated." This brings us to the year 1902, when he began to deliver the most noteworthy of his courses, on "The History of Political Ideas," and repeated it with constant changes until 1920. In 1924 he returned to the School to give one short course on "The Causes of the War in 1914"—one of the pieces of work preliminary to "The International Anarchy."

Since the London School of Economics is non-residential, there was little opportunity for social intercourse. He travelled up, gave his lecture in the afternoon or evening, held an informal class in connection with it, and then went back. But even such an arrangement as this leaves a mark when it continues for twenty-four years. Besides doing good there, he enlarged his experience, for he met students who were not as well off as their Cambridge contemporaries, and were less exclusively the products of Public Schools, and he also became acquainted with Indians and Chinese.

The titles of some of his Cambridge courses were: "Modern France" (1892), "The Transition to Democracy in Modern England" (1894–96), "The Machinery of Administration under Democracy" (1897), "The Theory of Law and Government" (1897–99), "Analytical and Deductive Politics" (1900 onwards). When he looks back at his lecturing both there and at London his summary is as follows:

My business was to enlarge and concretise my subject, which became, in fact, a general discussion of modern political problems. I came in time, I believe, to lecture well in the academic way. I spoke always from notes, added continually year after year to my matter, as was natural in a subject so continually developing, not to say bulging and obtruding outside all skins of general theory. I was interested myself, and I think I interested my pupils, most of them. At any rate my audience always continued to the end without any defalcations to speak of, and varied round about a hundred in the latter years. I had a quite definite idea of what I wanted to do in lectures—to stimulate the students' interest so that they should feel they were dealing with a live subject which was going to be of interest and practical importance to them all their life. I used not to conceal my own opinions, but also not to preach them unfairly, having in fact, in many important questions, a very open mind. I lectured in this way for some twenty-five years, never losing my own freshness and interest. Whether I produced any result, or what, who can say? The parable of the sower applies to all such work, and a single teacher is rather a light makeweight against family and social interests and preoccupations. Still I expect I helped to wake up some minds. What more can a teacher do, or what better?

Most people would say that he was really a great lecturer of his type. That type, as he is careful to point out, was the academic. Neither his matter nor his manner could move masses of people, and he believed indeed that it is impossible to touch men to any fineness when they are gathered into anything so clumsy as a mass. Towards the end he was a triumphantly successful broadcaster; he had the opportunity of

addressing numbers of individuals who remained individuals, an opportunity which no speaker has yet had
since the beginning of the world; and he was extending
his audience in this sense when he died. But except at
an election (for instance, at Scarborough in 1909), he
never addressed a crowd. His hatred of crowd-psycho-
logy was so great that he could scarcely bear to discuss
it, much less to utilize it; in fact it was too great, and
limited his utility; when two or three hundred were
gathered together, he felt too sure it was in the name
of the devil. And it must be remembered that he
believed in the devil—that is to say in the existence of
evil; it was one of the points on which he differed from
his more youthful audiences.

After his death one of his former London students con-
tributed this impression of him to the *Journal of Education*:

> We were an odd job lot at those evening classes!
> Clerks and students and teachers, young and old, men
> and women of all sorts and conditions; but he interested
> us all and aroused us in a truly wonderful way. He had
> no physical advantages except a charming smile and a
> very sensitive mouth. His voice was always husky
> though very pleasant to listen to, and he had none of
> the arts of the orator. But there was a distinction about
> his whole individuality that arrested attention and in
> some curious way kept his large class of not highly
> intellectual students, such as he lectured to in Cam-
> bridge, spellbound. I think perhaps we never knew
> what to expect and we never quite grasped his point of
> view. . . . He seemed now to be an aristocrat, now a
> thorough going democrat, so that often his class was
> left gasping. You went away to *think*—and that was, I
> suppose, what he wanted.

A sympathetic impression of his lecturing at Cambridge is to be found in Osbert Burdett's *The Art of Life*.

Lecturing, as he conceived it, was a thoughtful conversation. No reply was anticipated, but the speaker had to keep the naturalness and good manners of talk. So that the transition from the lecture hall to the class, in which his pupils did talk, was easy and welcome, and the transition from the class to luncheon or to a ride, where his pupils could both talk to him and lecture him, was easier still. He broke up the illiberal distinction between lessons and leisure which has done so much to cramp human development; hard work lay at one end of the scale, amusement at the other, but both required intelligence and sensitiveness, and were aspects of education. So continuously did he believe in education that he seldom used the word; it was the air breathed by the spirit of man, and if the air a man is breathing is resolved into its components, the result may be stimulating to experts, but the man himself dies.

Besides the classes held in connection with the lectures, he took the third and fourth year History men at King's in Essays. The sort of subjects he set were: Church and State, Machiavelli, Toleration, Malthus, Wells' "Utopia." When the essays came to be corrected it became apparent that, like all genuine educationalists, he did not teach for teaching's sake. He roped people in to get ideas on some problem which puzzled him, and so would talk more about the problem itself than about their treatment of it. This disconcerted his weaker pupils, who wanted to be shown where they went wrong, but his indifference to their heresies was counterbalanced by his severity over their style. "It hasn't come yet," he would say. He knew very well when sentences went wrong, had no patience with the "mot injuste," which often seems so marvellous to the young, and came down, perhaps rather too heavily, on the side of limpidity and logic. How good is his own prose style? He was at that time disciplining it and paring away "beauties," so that it might respond better to the movements of his thought.

From his classes and essay-talks we slide onwards into social intercourse and hospitality, and this is the moment when I want to introduce myself.

I first met him in 1898. A friend of his father's and of my aunt's had asked him to be kind, so he invited me to lunch. We had Winchester cutlets, a sort of elongated rissole to which he was then addicted, but I can remember nothing about the conversation, and probably there was none. Impressions get so mixed; but I recall him as sadder and older than he appeared to be fifteen years later. He knew nothing about me—there was nothing to know—and I had never heard of him. His rooms were on staircase H of Gibbs, ground-floor—the staircase nearest the chapel—and we sat alone in the large front room silently eating the cutlets and drinking the reddish-brown sauce in which they lay. The food was less good than it became in later years, the host shyer, the guest shyer still, and I departed unprepossessing and unprepossessed. A few weeks later I asked him to lend me a play which had a great vogue among my fellow freshmen. I forget its name. He handed it to me gloomily, and asked when I brought it back what I thought of it. I replied nervously that I was afraid I didn't think it so very good. His face lit up. "No, of course it's no good," he said. This lighting up of the face was a thing to watch for. It meant that he had seen something which must vaguely be called "life," and it brought life to anyone who saw it. It was part of what—vaguely again—must be called his charm. Charm, in most men and nearly all women, is a decoration. It genuinely belongs to them, as a good complexion may, but it lies on the surface and can vanish. Charm in Dickinson was structural. It penetrated and upheld everything he did, it remained into old age, and I saw it first that afternoon at the end of last century, when he was only thirty-five, and when I kindled him by managing to be honest over a trifle. The "lighting up" really belonged to a greater occasion than this—to the entrance into the room of a friend. Then he would emerge from his inner life with a smile, which made him for the moment indescribably beautiful.

He photographed well, so that I need not try to describe his features. The complexion was not good, the head bowed a little forward from the shoulders when he walked, though the shoulders themselves, like the body generally, were shapely and strong. The hands were large. The clothes, except during the American visits, erred on the dowdy side—dark blue serges, shirts of indistinction, podgy ties. I dress like that myself, except for illogical flashinesses, and once when I invited him to accompany me into one of these he replied that it is hopeless to dress well unless one's personal appearance corresponds. This made me realize that he was at all events not contented with his own appearance. I did not understand why. There was a beauty about him which cannot be given that patronizing label "spiritual," a beauty which, though it had nothing to do with handsomeness, did belong to the physical, so that his presence was appropriate amid gorgeous scenery or exquisite flowers. The portrait of him by Roger Fry features a sumptuous costume, which is not typical but it is satisfactory that he should have been obliged to wear it once.

I did not see much of him while I was an undergraduate and when in my fourth year I turned from classics to history and planned to go to him for essays I was dished by Oscar Browning, who said: "You're not coming to me at all, you must come to me." So once a fortnight I read aloud about Wallenstein or Louis XIV to the handkerchiefs which covered O.B.'s face, and Dickinson's power to teach remained unknown to me, except as far as I have heard of it from others. I belonged to his "Discussion Society," however. He had founded it in 1904 as the result of some popular lectures on philosophy which had been delivered by McTaggart. It was a blend between the type of society described in an earlier chapter and the tuitional type presided over by a don. Dickinson presided but there was freedom for the rank and file. The papers I forget, with the exception of one on Sex, read by George Barger (now Professor of Chemistry at Edinburgh). Sex was not mentioned at Cambridge in those days—that is to say not in the small circle I knew —and there were some high anticipations about Barger's paper, and some care on Dickinson's part to ensure that only seriously minded youths should attend. The paper was statistical, the discussion stilted, the evening interminable, yet I recall it as an example of his sensitiveness and tact; he knew just how large a stone it is wise to drop into the pond.

The above trifles may show how consistent his influence was, and how it could penetrate unpromising material. "I think of him," writes Dominick Spring-Rice, "at the queer society he ran in which you drew lots as to your turn for speaking and had to tell what you believed was the truth; standing, at the end, in front of the fireplace, rubbing himself and saying clearly for each of us what in our muddled way we could not say clearly for ourselves." Teaching, to him, was a process which transcended any formula and went on at all times, and it could not be distinguished, in the final analysis, from being taught. By the end of his life he had become so wise that he was able to learn from the young. His affection for them and his desire to help them were joined with a much rarer quality: respect. "Maxima debetur pueris reverentia?" No, certainly not. It was not that type of respect. It was a recognition that the young may instruct the old.

Financially his lectureships enabled him to live and to write books, and since the college considerately let him confine his teaching to the two winter terms, he was left with the Summer Term and the Long Vacation for creative work, "an arrangement which no commission would ever approve; it slipped through under the freedom of the old Cambridge." Before coming to the books themselves we must glance at his general attitude towards the university, the university for which he entertained such high and unusual hopes, as the letter quoted at the beginning of this chapter testifies.

His love of Cambridge was touched with fear. He only trusted her in so far as she is the city of youth. For him the undergraduate is the true owner of the University, and the dons exist for the purpose of inducting him into his kingdom. Having taken his degree there, he passes out into life, bringing with him standards of conduct and memories of affection and beauty which cannot be elsewhere obtained. Cambridge did this much for Dickinson, and she did it through him for dozens, perhaps hundreds, of young men who now mourn his memory. "An unspoilt youth of twenty with his mind just waking up and his feelings all fresh and open to good is the most beautiful thing this world produces," he writes to Mrs Webb, and Cambridge shared with Ancient Athens the maieutic power which brings such minds into the light. The Cephissus flows with the Cam through this city by the great lawn of King's under the bridge of Clare, towards plane trees which have turned into the chestnuts of Jesus. Ancient and modern unite through the magic of youth.

But there was another Cambridge which filled him with dismay and which he connected less with the scenery than with the weather: the Cambridge of the organizing and the researching don. Stuffy yet raw, parochial yet colourless—what a city was this! What a hole! Schoolmasters paraded its streets, specialists riddled its walls, governesses, married to either, held their lugubrious courts in its suburbs. Here the east wind blows for ever and the mist never lifts off the mud. Yes, he dreaded the increasing fuss and rush of university business, not for selfish reasons but because it tended to neglect the needs of the individual undergraduate and to keep him in the position of a child, children being more easily managed. And he mistrusted research even more, although it is in itself so admirable and so necessary, because research atrophies the mind and renders it incapable of human intercourse: "the spectacle of learning gets more depressing to me every year," he tells Mrs Webb, "I care only for fruitful and vital handling of the eternal commonplaces or else for a new insight that will really help some one to internal freedom." If the schoolmaster teaches wrongly, the specialist cannot teach at all, and between the two of them what room is left for Socrates?

There is something to be said against his views, as he realized, and there is a third Cambridge whose existence he forgot—the agglomeration conveniently known as "the varsity" which takes pass-degrees, roars round football fields, sits down in the middle of Hammersmith Broadway after the boat race, and covers actresses with soot. Silly and idle young men did not come his way, no more did hearties and toughs unless they had intellectual leanings. This was due partly to his own constitution and partly to that of King's, which only admits men who are reading for honours and does not duck an intellectual in the fountain oftener than once in twenty years, apologizing elaborately to him afterwards. In its exquisite enclosure a false idea can be gained of enclosures outside though not of the infinite verities. Dickinson, pacing up and down with his arms behind him, kept in touch in his own fashion with the world, but he could never slap it on the back or stand it a drink. And he loathed its brutality and bullying—with them there could be no compromise; his objection to rowdiness was not its noise but its inability to flourish without a victim.

Essentially a college man, he did not take much part in University affairs. The chief occasion was in 1903, when at the invitation of Professor Marshall he helped to form the new Economics Tripos. Economics had hitherto been inadequately included in the History course. Realizing its importance in modern life, he sought separate recognition. What interested him though was not economics proper, not the laws of supply and demand, not the mathematics of wealth, but the reaction of men to material surroundings and their attempts to improve them. He held that the study of recent history and of political institutions could help them here, and it was as an advocate of his special subject, Political Science, that he joined forces with Professor Marshall. He became a member of the "Economics and Political Science Syndicate" which was appointed to report to the Senate. In the ensuing debate he made a short and effective speech, in reply to the pure historians. He regretted that everyone could not know everything, and especially that historians could not know the whole of history, but pointed out that there is a profitable alternative in the analytical method, which studies causes and effects among co-existent phenomena. When the new tripos was established, he became the first Secretary of the Economics Board.

His other university activities are not important. When it came to a vote at the Senate House he was on the side of freedom, but freedom is a word variously applied. We find him for instance in 1898 voting against recognizing a Roman Catholic lodging house as a hostel, on the ground that any institution recognized by the University ought to be free to all creeds. Henry Sidgwick and others of his friends voted for recognition, on the ground that Roman Catholics ought to be free to have a hostel. In 1902 he voted for the abolition of compulsory Greek ("disliking the word 'compulsory'," comments one of his classical friends, "and not seeing 'Greek' came after it"). And he assisted in the unchaining of women, but without enthusiasm. His suicidal sense of fairness left him no alternative here. If women wanted a degree or a vote or anything else which men monopolized, it was his duty to help them to get it, even if they overwhelmed him afterwards. There were a few women to whom he was devoted and a few to whom he would have confidently entrusted the destiny of mankind, but he was not a really creditable feminist. He did think that men on the whole are superior. "Oh dear, what is to happen to them?" he once murmured sadly as a stream of aspiring and uninspiring spinsters flowed round the front court of King's; "I don't know and they don't know." And then in still lower tones as if his bookshelves might overhear him, "Oh dear! What they want is a husband!" These were his unregenerate thoughts. At other times he remembered the cruelty and parsimony of the Victorian girl's upbringing and felt that no restitution could be too generous, and there exist among his manuscripts a few pages of a fantasy about Héloise and a Chorus of Cats which is conceived in this spirit of atonement.

From "Goldsworthy Lowes Dickinson"

A gentle, unassuming sort of prose: but very direct, very lucid, and even where most colloquial perfectly fitting. Prose like this is far more difficult to write than the untroubled manner suggests. It comes of self-knowledge and inner poise; it comes from the free play of the mind, the care for clarity and detachment that Dickinson and his friends also stood for. You find another aspect of it in the work of the philosopher G. E. Moore, to whom Mr Forster refers a little later; his "Principia Ethica" (C.U.P.) and his little book on "Ethics" (H.U.L.) are fine examples of patient clarity in definition, argument and discussion. It is not the only source of power in Mr Forster's own novels (where his best prose is to be found) but it is an important source. Both for their prose and their passion, the first "Where Angels fear to tread" and the last "A Passage to India" (Arnold) offer the best reward. "A Passage to India" and "Howard's End" have appeared as Penguin books.

To the Greater Glory of God
Eric Gill

*This comes from the "Autobiography" of Eric Gill,
who was born at Brighton in 1882 and died in London
in 1940. He writes of his life as the father of a family and
as a craftsman, and he takes up (in terms of practical
living) that rejection of the modern environment and the
modern way of life that D. H. Lawrence expressed in
'Nottingham and the Mining Country.' He was received
into the Roman Catholic Church, with his wife and three
children, in 1913: for here, he felt, was the church of the
oldest Christian tradition, the most total alternative
to "the essential dirtiness, dirtiness in its very being
and nature, of the industrial capitalist world." His life
became one of submission to the rule of God, a submission expressed by membership as a tertiary in the
Dominican Order of Preachers; his way of looking
at the modern world, and the exercise of his gifts, sprang
directly from his sacramental faith.*

*A paragraph from the last pages of the "Auto-
biography" can best introduce the prose that follows:*

*The marvellous feats of our mechanized 'scientific'
industrial world are not human feats. They are no
more than the feats of highly intelligent animals and
the more we perfect our mechanization so much the more
nearly do we approach the impersonal life of bees or ants.
And if I might attempt to state in one paragraph the
work which I have chiefly tried to do in my life it is this:*

to make a cell of good living in the chaos of our world.
Lettering, type-designing, engraving, stone-carving, draw-
ing—these things are all very well, they are means to the
service of God and of our fellows and therefore to the
earning of a living, and I have earned my living by them.
But what I hope above all things is that I have done
something towards re-integrating bed and board, the
small farm and the workshop, the home and the school,
earth and heaven.

This book was completed during some of the darkest
months of the Second World War.

Adam sinned when he fell from contemplation'—
when he saw the treasures of this world as things
ministering to *him*. We may recover something of our
lost equanimity, our lost integrity, our lost innocence
when, instead of seeing things as things to be grasped
and possessed, we see them as beings manifesting
Being himself.

I need only add that there is a real connection between contemplation and material quietness. The driver
of a locomotive must, in duty bound, keep his eyes
fixed constantly and without wavering upon the line
ahead and the signals and must at the same time bear
in mind the gradients and the pressure gauges. . . . Yet
in his mind quietness may rule. So it is in any life, even
in the turmoil of domesticity—most disturbing of all
hectic disturbances. It remains true that in a general
way we need physical quiet if we are to attain to
quietude. In that respect life at Capel-y-ffin was a quiet
life. Troubles there were all of our own making and

we were not disturbed by the constant petty feverish-
ness of what they are pleased to call civilization in the
towns.

I wish I could write a special book all about our four
years in the Black Mountains. I did not intend ever to
leave Capel, I did not anticipate any reason for doing
so. The distance from Bedlem Hospital was no hard-
ship and made no serious difficulties to my work, so
from my point of view there was no reason for moving
—moreover I couldn't imagine how we could ever face
so big a job. It had been bad enough moving from
Sussex, but now there was another four years of
accumulation. . . . It was a good life and it was a marvellous training for the girls. For the great thing about
it was that we were compelled by mere geographical
circumstance to live in a way which would have been
fantastically heroic and unnatural and pedantic in any
place less remote from industrial civilization. *We had*
to do our transport by pony and pony cart. *We had* to
bake our own bread—we couldn't possibly have
bought enough loaves and got them from the shop.
And all our neighbours were doing the same. We were
not, as we should have been at, say, Wimbledon, living
according to some theory, however excellent, derived
from a study of Cobbett's *Cottage Economy*. They could
use that excellent book as being what for them it
actually was, an up-to-date textbook. We got coal
fairly easily from the Welsh coal pits, but we burned
a lot of wood which we cut from our own plantation.
We did a lot of our own building repairs. The mistress
and the girls parcelled the home-work between them.
The eldest daughter managed the animals and the

farm. Their mother did the baking and the two younger ones did the house and the cooking—but of course they all helped with everything. I don't reckon that I myself did much to help. I had too much engraving and carving to do, but I was occasionally more help than hindrance. I say it was a good life, and it was, and it was a natural life. And Donald Attwater, who was an excellent glazier in the intervals when he wasn't editing dictionaries or writing about Uniat Eastern Churches, repaired all the lead windows, of which there were dozens.

And we bathed naked all together in the mountain pools and under the waterfalls. And we had heavenly picnics by the Nant-y-buch in little sunny secluded paradises, or climbed the green mountains and smelt the smell of a world untouched by men of business. But alas! that is saying too much, for the evil hand, the outstretched claw of the dealer and financier was bringing ruin all around. The valley, the lovely vale of Ewyas, was never afflicted with his evil presence—his petrol pumps and road-houses, his factory filth and his suburban vulgarity. But his evil influence was over all. The population of the valley was but a quarter of what it had been fifty years before. There were twenty ruined cottages between Capel-y-ffin and Llanthony four miles lower down the valley. The young men had gone to the mines and were wandering unemployed in the Rhondda, their fathers could not call them home for the city of London found it more profitable to foster Australian Capitalist sheep farming than to preserve the thousand-year traditions of the South Wales mountains. We were living in a dying land—unspoiled but dying. It is still the same paradise and it is possible that it will long remain so. For by the mercy of geographical accident all the valleys are cul-de-sacs. Let the industrial-capitalist disease do its worst—the Black Mountains of Brecon will remain untouched and their green valleys lead nowhere. God help them! I hope I am right.

And while we lived at Capel we had a great adventure in the south of France. A dear friend bought a small house at Salies-de-Béarn and we conceived the project of sharing it with her. She bought the house and we furnished it. Certainly it was an adventure and I count it among the influential things. You see we didn't just go there for a holiday, we went and lived there all one winter. I can't imagine how one does such things. I suppose if you've got an enthusiastic mistress and three enthusiastic daughters it's not so impossible; but looking back on the affair I wonder we undertook it.

This experience was of course perfectly in harmony with our life at Capel. The great difference was that the French life was vastly more cultured. It was as though Capel were our kitchen and Salies our salon. And we had the experience, nowhere obtainable in England, of living not only in a civilized town, but a civilized *life* also! Chichester is a civilized town, but it scarcely knows a civilized life. Lincoln's Inn was, in its domestic and semi-collegiate way, a civilized life but it was not a *town* life. There is now no civilized town life in England. It has all long since been submerged in the universal vulgarity of our commercialism. Perhaps the English have never enjoyed such a thing. Maybe our climate has not that benevolence which makes such serenity possible. I do not know—though it is difficult to believe that the beauty and spaciousness of such towns as Beaconsfield and Amersham were not the product of a way of living similarly beautiful and spacious. I say I do not know. What is certain is that life, the town life, in such small places as Salies-de-Béarn, has a quality of goodness and quietness and even holiness which seems to have gone for ever from England.

And this brings me to a matter which I am much concerned in and yet one which is more than most things difficult to describe with justice and balance. We have been so accustomed to the thought that though our very life depends upon the work of our industrial towns, yet that when we seek peace and love-liness we cannot expect them to give it. We take it for granted that beauty "resides" in the country. The country, thinks the townsman, may be boring but it is certainly beautiful. Life and all the interest of life is in the town, but no one would say that modern towns are beautiful. For the most part the townsman is quite happy to let beauty go. He likes a day or a week or two in the country for a holiday. He will subscribe to societies which make it their business to preserve "beauty spots." He picnics in thousands at Burnham Beeches. He founds the National Trust and the Society for the Preservation of Rural Industries (God help him), and his Office of Works spends a lot of money patching up and propping up the ruins of medieval castles and monasteries. But all that sort of thing is not vital to him. It's on the same level as the picture galleries and museums which have taken the place of cathedrals in his towns. He is persuaded that they are important and he has a sort of sentimental veneration for them, but that they have no real importance for him is proved conclusively by the fact that he does nothing whatever to conform his own life to the principles and beliefs which were the inspiration of the pre-industrial world—on the contrary he, with monotonous enthusiasm and energy, continues to develop the commercial-industrialism which is in its nature destructive of all that he thus pays to preserve from disappearance, and which is rapidly destroying the very land itself.

And from one point of view the townsman is right. It *is* a lot of nonsense all this cackle about the beauty of the country. And the cackle would never have been heard if the towns had not become such monsters of indecency and indignity. The right and proper and natural development of human life unsullied by an insubordinate commercialism no more leads to ugly towns than to an ugly countryside. On the contrary, the town properly thought of is the very crown and summit of man's creativeness and should be the vehicle for the highest manifestations of his sensibility, his love of order and seemliness, of dignity and loveliness. Man collaborates with God in creating—that, physically speaking, is what he is for. The natural world, following without the slightest deviation, the line of least resistance, blooms in a million million marvels of natural beauty. The beauty of flowers and trees and beasts and insects, the beauty of bones and muscles and crystals and clouds, is the product of this unswerving but unconscious obedience. Man alone among created things can resist: man alone can willingly obey. Man alone can give thanks: man alone can respond and take a conscious and willing part in the universal creativity. Thus, properly thought of, man's works, alone of all material things, can have the spiritual qualities of tenderness and love, of humour and gaiety: and they alone can, on the other hand, have the qualities of wickedness and pride and silliness.

> Man indeed, one part of thy creation, has the will to praise thee: yes, man, though he bears his mortality about with him, even man has the will to praise thee . . . thou dost stir him up, that it may delight him to praise thee, for thou hast made us for thyself and our hearts are restless till they find rest in thee. . . .

These words from the first page of the first and greatest autopsychography, by one of those miracles of coincidence, came into my hand just while I was pondering on what I had just written. I am but echoing their thought—man is that part of creation which can praise his creator. Because he can, he is ordained to do so; and because he is so ordained he is in misery unless he obeys the call.

Now it is right and salutary that we praise God in our hearts—singing canticles. It is no less right that we should praise him in the work of our hands. In its dumb way all creation praises him—*omnia opera benedicite Domino, benedicite omnia germinantia in terra Domino*. Then shall other things praise him and only man keep silence? And as it is in their very springing and germinating that all living things praise him how can it be said that man's works alone need not do so?

Obviously I am only writing down rhetorical questions. There is no possible answer but that in the work of his hands man, without any pride or exaggeration of his powers, can add to and indeed improve upon, and that to a literally infinite degree, the creatures of inanimate nature.

The point that I am thus struggling to reach is that clear and heavenly as is the beauty of the Natural world, clear and heavenly as are the mountains and the seas, the forests and the flowers and all the animal world, even when, yes indeed, even when most "red in tooth and claw," nevertheless the cultivated fields, the farms, the roads, the villages are, when they are the works of men in peace and charity, infinitely more beautiful. And if that be so, the towns and cities where men foregather in the same peace and charity should be and have been and may be again more beautiful still.

I have said that I have a special predilection for texts referring to the heavenly Jerusalem and of course I place as leader among such texts the one which says: *Jerusalem which is built as a city.* I fled from the bedlam of London to discover the lost Bethlehem. But I could not forget that text. Heaven, man's final beatitude, is likened to a place and that place a city. It is not true that the town's primary reason of existence is to serve the countryside, though it must and does do so. The truth is the converse; the countryside exists to support and uphold and nourish and maintain the city. It is only in our gross betrayal of our calling to a house not made with hands that the English town has become a shambles and a brothel and a place of filth and disease. Thus the call to the land, to the earth, is the necessary first call. We must be born again and we must be born again on the land, to dig the earth, to plant and cultivate, to be shepherds and swineherds, to hew wood and draw water, to build simple dwellings and simple places of prayer. But we need not therefore be blinded to what is the truth. Because Babylon is vile it does not follow that Jerusalem is vile also.

I had some such thoughts as these when we fled from London in 1907. I had them even more strongly and consciously when in 1924 we left Ditchling and the community, "the city" on which we had set such hopes, and fled again, fled to the remotest place we could find. And this is the point I have been trying to get to, I have actually now got to it, about Salies-de-Béarn. At last, at last we had the chance to live for a time in a human city which was in some sort a holy city, and to live a life, a city life which was a holy life. Holy, Holy, Holy, and that means hale and hearty and whole and healthy with a mind set heavenwards. I exaggerate; of course I exaggerate. The little town in the foothills of the Pyrenees would be astonished to hear itself called holy. Was it not "run" by its local politicians? Had it not got one of the worst possible memorials of "the Great War" with its cock crowing on the front? Was there not the hideous half-built hotel—the building abandoned because the "company" went bankrupt? Was not the parish church almost falling down and was not the "altar of Repose" on Good Friday an almost incredible monstrosity of lace and frills? Were not such new buildings as there were as bad as any in Birmingham or Edinburgh? Alas! the answer is "yes" in every case. And yet it represented and I was properly justified in thinking so the holy city.

The great thing was that I had a job of work to do —it was about sixty engravings for the Golden Cockerel edition of Chaucer's *Troilus and Creseyde*. I had an excellent room over a chemist's shop (Bourdagubelle—but perhaps I haven't spelt it rightly) just round the corner from the *Place*. After Mass at the Parish Church of St Vincent I used to go to the café in the *Place* for Little Breakfast and then to my work till lunch time. Home to the villa for lunch and then back to work till dusk. Generally one or more of the girls would come to meet me and we went to Benediction on the way home to supper. Often in the evenings we went down to the town and sat outside the café in the *Place* or the café de la Terasse beside the little river, and sipped the local liqueur. Sometimes there would be a concert at the parish school. Day after day passed thus, as beautifully regular and reliable as a good clock. On feast-days we had holidays and we made expeditions—to Sauveterre with its terrace café a hundred feet above the rushing Gave, to St Engrace, right up in the pass, to Bellocq, to Oloron Ste Marie where there is one of the best and most vehement sculptures in the world, but especially to Sauveterre because it was within walking distance and after a day by the river it was nice to walk the five miles home (with a good swill of red wine, sitting on the bench outside the Estaminet at the top of the hill) in the cool of the evening singing songs along the road. (I haven't told you this: singing songs was one of their special things; they knew simply hundreds of songs and sang them in trio—if we were at home I used to play accompaniments, not always too successfully, on the tin whistle—songs of England and Scotland, the Highlands, the Hebrides, of Ireland and France, a never-ending succession, one reminding of and leading to another and what one didn't remember another would. Did ever anyone ever before have three such daughters?) Once we went to Lourdes—of which the less said the better (but there is no doubt about the Grotto). And once we went to Peyrehorade to buy pots. And once we went as far as Bayonne because I wanted to buy an oil stove and couldn't get one at Salies. And once we spent the week-end at Fuenterrabia and thus poked our noses into Spain. (It was Palm Sunday and the children came in from all the country round carrying branches of trees so that the big church was filled with greenery and you could only just see little faces of children peeping out between the leaves. And with no other human audience, because the lazy grown-ups had all been to the low Mass at eight, a small choir of men sang, and very admirably, all Vittoria's music of the Passion. Well!). And our little son went to school at the parish school and learned to talk French like a native (though the accent of those parts is not Parisian) and to appreciate the fact that it is possible to describe the battle of Waterloo without mentioning the name of Wellington. . . . And there was the saintly Marie who cooked for us, and cooked like an angel or perhaps simply like a good French woman. They learnt a lot from her; moreover, as I said before, she was a saint. Well, that is Salies-de-Béarn.

But there is one thing more I must try to describe

because it influenced me very much. I went one day with Elizabeth ——, the dear friend with whom we shared the villa, to a farm at Castanniede to see her old friends there (she had had her baby there twenty years before) and we were asked to dinner. It was a big farm owned and worked by the family—grandfather, sons and daughters and their children. But the old grandfather was past work and almost past life. He sat in the chimney corner with his cap on and dribbled. And he more or less minded the baby in the cradle at his feet and the baby dribbled too. Poor old man, the former head of all things, but now fading out in second childhood and scolded and mouth-wiped like the child at his feet (in England he would have been in the workhouse, looked after kindly enough but by paid strangers). And round the table in the big long kitchen-living-room was the huge family. The farmer and his wife and their grown-up sons and daughters and the younger children—down to little boys and girls only just big enough to sit up to table. I think there must have been a married grandson and his wife and children —how else account for such young babies about? And we had, in honour, I think, of the visit of Elizabeth to her old friends, the most sumptuous and tremendous feed. All the food was off the farm—the meat, the vegetables, the bread, the cakes, the wine and finally the *petits verres* of their own cognac. It was a grand example of the patriarchal home and the self-sufficing farm—a grand example of human life in all its vigour and feebleness, its joy and pathos. The two extremes of feebleness, the decrepit slobbery old man trembling and mumbling by the fire with the tiny baby six months old, and, in between, all the grandeurs of human strength and will and courage, the capable craftsmanship of the women and girls, the humble and handsome men hard-worn with the work and the weather —who all disappeared before we finished the vast amount we were expected to eat, to go about their various jobs on the farm. How could I help comparing it with our poor decayed English farm life? How could I help comparing it with the life in our modern towns, the slum life, the suburban life, the life in our smart new blocks of flats? The self-sufficiency and self-reliance of the southern farm, the feeble dependence and sycophancy of the wretched crowds of wage-slaves and money grubbers. Such reflections would lead only to despair but for the heartening fact that it is *our* civilization that is doomed, not theirs. It is of the very nature of our life that we should destroy ourselves —either in mutual murder or in physical and territorial barrenness. But the essence and actuality of their life is creativeness and fruitfulness and peace.

And there is one admirable and, as it were, heraldic symbol of that good life which I like to ponder on, for it typifies and sums up the whole difference between that life and ours and that is the ox-drawn wagon. In this particular period of our history wherein we and all our kind have made speed our very God, it must seem not only eccentric but even blasphemous so to think. "No man ever hurries except when catching flies," says the Arab proverb. And in our industrial world everyone is hurrying and no one is catching anything but flies. It is not only a fever; it is a fever of futility. It is a madness; and, like all madness it means nothing and leads to death. And that, I suppose is why the yoked oxen are so heavenly lovely; they are quiet —like the "still small voice"; they are slow—like the germination of seeds; they are patient—like the earth. And so they are a symbol of fruitfulness; for it is said of them that hear the word and keep it; that they "bring forth fruit in *patience*."

And in the middle of all this agricultural righteousness there was the little town with its little *Place*, overshadowed by green trees, its lovely houses and its little river. It is more than a market town, though it is also that. It is more than a health resort to which people come to bathe in the salt water, though it is that too. It is the centre of worships—the church in which we confess the fatherhood of God and the streets and meeting places in which we confess the brotherhood of men. That I think is why the country must be said to exist to support the town; because the town is the symbol of that heavenly Jerusalem in which men unite to praise God and to love one another. In the town it becomes a corporate praise and a corporate love. But it depends upon righteousness. The country does not exist to support Babylons but *holy* cities—when we say that the country exists to serve the town, God forbid that it should be supposed that we mean it exists to serve London and Birmingham . . . such places are not towns in any human or holy sense.

Nevertheless the salvation of England cannot be brought about by town improvements; it can only come by the land. The town, the holy city, is nourished upon elements drawn from the soil. The modern towns of our industrial England have no such nourishment.

They draw their galvanic twitchings and palpitations (for you can hardly call it life) from machines. The modern town is a warren of business men. And though it is still dependent upon the country, it does not desire to be so; for it is slowly but surely turning agriculture into a mechanical or even a merely chemical industry. It will therefore not die only of mass murder (such as is going on this very day as I write—in London and Berlin . . .) and barrenness but also of poisoning. It will die anyway. So our business is to get back on to the land as quickly as possible.

And that was Salies-de-Béarn. Our longest stay was that winter of 1926 and 1927. Since then we made several similar visits—in fact I've jumbled them all up together in my account of the first—but Salies in its turn became a thing of the past; for I don't see how we can ever get there again. Our dear friend is dead and the villa is sold and all our nice furniture with it. It remains alive in my memory—may the Lord preserve it in the flesh.

I have said that Salies-de-Béarn was to Capel-y-ffin as salon to kitchen. Our expeditions to the south of France were just like going to the family sitting-room after the day's work. We reclined at our ease and, of course without saying anything about it, we contemplated the divine mysteries. It *was* like that. If there had been anything comparable in our native land we should have had no need to take all that immence trouble. Just imagine it! From South Wales and, to start with, fifteen miles to the station; then to London, then to Paris, then the night journey and half the next day. (But the midday Bock at Puyon was worth all the weary hours between Paris and Bordeaux and through the Landes. . . . But on one occasion I remember arguing, or what not, nearly all the night with David Jones and that helped us through the journey—much to the annoyance, I fear, of our fellow travellers who wished to sleep—but how absurd of them!) I don't *want* to go abroad. I don't *want* to go to the south of France to find a human life. But I want to find a human life. And if I can't find it nearer than a thousand miles away, a thousand miles I'll have to go. And it's not merely for myself. I'm burning with desire that my *children* shall know and desire the good. That was what turned the scale—that *they* might be well fed.

And, thank goodness, it worked—you have only to ask them. But we had to go to the south of France to find what we wanted in one way just as we had had to go to the Black Mountains to find what we wanted in the other. And just as Salies came to an end, so did Capel-y-ffin—as our life in Sussex had done.

From "Autobiography"

That is a prose whose buoyancy of rhythm, unconstraint, and verve suggest not only the quality of the man but also the tested vitality of his faith and practice. It affirms the value of worthwhile work, of imaginative living, of the person and the family and the community, and resists the drives and the more subtle pressures of modern 'civilization.' So in some degree it is a prose of protest, oddly direct and unconventional; it matches his direct cast of mind and his wholeheartedness.

Eric Gill's prose was not the most important part of

his life's work, but if you enjoy its straightforward tang
it can best be savoured (after the "Autobiography") in
"Last Essays" and "In a Strange Land" (Cape). He
expresses his convictions more deliberately in "The
Necessity of Belief" (Faber and Faber) and "Christianity
and the Machine Age" (Sheldon). His work in stone is
widely distributed through Britain. His carving can be
studied at Westminster Cathedral or the underground
station at St James's Park. He designed eleven faces of
printing type, and made wood engravings for books of the
Golden Cockerel Press. Some may care to explore further
the ideas about landscape, village, and town in the Britain
of yesterday and today that both D. H. Lawrence and Eric
Gill affirm so vigorously. They may be directed to "Tomorrow's Landscape" by Sylvia Crowe, to "Outrage" and
to "Counter-attack," all published by Architectural Press;
and to the pamphlet "Your England" published for the
journal "The Use of English" by Chatto and Windus.

The Fine Art
George Sturt

These two short chapters from "The Wheelwright's Shop" (first published in 1923) connect the present with the past. They give us the kind of living Eric Gill envisaged; only here the dignity and delicacy of daily work and the self-respect and sense of fulfilment it brought to daily life, flower from an older world: the village community of agricultural Britain. George Sturt was born in 1863 and died in 1927. He is the closest, shrewdest and wisest observer of our rural world. He was the son of a Farnham wheelwright, and after a period away from it—just long enough to help him gain detachment and perspective—he took over the family business, living in a nearby village. He set himself as a writer to know thoroughly the life and work about him and to elucidate its importance in a changing world. He looked both back to the traditions of workmanship and fellowship of an earlier age, and forward, with the Fabian movement, to an enlargement of the scope of village life, to worthier living conditions and more fitting prosperity.

Here he first describes with minute attention one facet of the wheelwright's craft—enough to suggest how imagination, intelligence, the human sense of fitness, the conscience itself, all play their part; then, in the person of Cook, one instance of the kind of personal life and attitude, dignified, self-possessed and quiet, that went with such daily work as this. You will find nothing sentimental, or slurred, or veiled here.

I

OF the stock (the nave or hub) I hardly dare speak, such a fine product it was, and so ignorant about it do I feel. It is true I learnt to buy stocks with confidence in my own judgment: I seasoned them, chopped them into shape, chose them at last even to satisfy Cook. Nay, he occasionally asked my opinion, if anything dubious was discovered in working. But, as I had never enough skill of hand and eye myself, I always entrusted the actual turning and mortising of stocks to a trusty man—Cook as long as he lived, and after him preferably Hole. These men, I knew, would sooner have been discharged than work badly, against their own conscience. So I left the stocks to them, only liking to look at each stock when it was brought from the lathe, and to "weight" it (poise it) in my arms and hear the wheelwright say "rare stock that." His enthusiasm was catching. I felt a glow of pride in having ministered, however humbly, to so noble a tradition. Then I left the stock again to the workman.

A lumpish cylinder in shape—eleven or twelve inches in diameter and twelve or thirteen inches from end to end—a newly-turned stock was a lovely thing —to the eyes, I thought, but more truly to sentiment, for the associations it hinted at. Elm from hedgerow or park, it spoke of open country. Well seasoned, it was a product of winter labour, of summer care in my own loft under my own hands. Long quiet afternoons it had lain there, where I could glance from the stocks across the town to the fields and the wooded hills.

I had turned it over and over, had chopped the bark away, had brushed off the mildew while the quiet winter darkness had stolen through the shed, and at last I had chosen the stock for use, and put it into Cook's hands.

And now it lay, butter-coloured, smooth, slightly fragrant, soon to begin years of field-work, after much more skill—the skill of ancient England—had been bestowed on it, though already telling of that skill in every curve. Certainly we did not consciously remember all these matters at the time: rather we concerned ourselves with the utility this block of elm would have, with its grip for many years of the oak spokes to be driven into it by and by. But, without thinking, we felt the glamour of the strong associations; and the skilled craftsmen must have felt it more than I, because they lived in that glamour as fishes live in water. They knew, better than any other may do, the answer of the elm when the keen blade goes searching between its molecules. This was, this is, for ever out of my reach. Only, I used to get some fellow-feeling about it, looking at a newly turned stock. I understood its parts—the shallow hollows at back and front where the blacksmith would presently put on the bonds, the sloping "nose," the clean chisel-cut of the "breast stroke." This list was cut in all round the stock to mark where the face of the spokes was to be.

So, when I had had my look, the wheel-maker—Cook or another—carried the stock to his bench, there to mark on it with straddling compasses the place for the first auger-holes, preliminary to mortising it for the spokes. A tricky job, this. One young man,

I remember, marking out his stock, prepared for an odd number of spokes—eleven or thirteen; though, every felloe requiring two, the spokes were always in even numbers; which error he did not detect until he had bored his stock and spoilt it. Too big for the fire, and too cross-grained to be easily split and thrown away, it lay about for months, an eyesore to the luckless youth who had spoilt it and a plain indication that it is not quite easy to mark a stock correctly.

Likewise was it not altogether a simple thing, though the skilled man seemed to find it easy enough, to fix the wobbly stock down for working upon. It was laid across a "wheel-pit"—a narrow trench with sills, about three feet deep—where iron clamps, themselves tightly wedged into the sills, held the stock steady back and front. Then the mortices were started, with auger-holes. How easy it looked! In my childhood I had heard the keen auger biting into the elm, had delighted in the springy spiral borings taken out; but now I learnt that only a strong and able man could make them.

The holes being bored, and before the actual mortising could begin, a gauge was attached to the front end of the stock, to be a guide for the coming operations. This gauge was a slender bar of wood—almost a lath—swinging round like one hand of a clock, but extending three feet or so beyond the stock. At the outer end of it a thin sliver of whalebone projected just so far as the front of the spokes would come if they had the right "dish." Note that. The spokes would have to lean forward a little bit; and the gauge was set so that this might be attended to even in mortising the stock. Before ever a spoke was actually put in the wheelwright tested the place for it, shutting one eye and squinting down with the other to see that the front edge of the mortice was properly in line with the whalebone sticking out from the gauge. The principle was very much like a marksman's taking his aim by foresight and backsight. One mortice having been cut, the stock was levered round with an iron bar so that the opposite mortice could be cut, and thus it was done all round, splinters or borings often dropping clear, right through the stock from one side to the other into the wheel-pit. The uncut ribs of wood left between the mortices were called "meshes"—a word that will be wanted again. I do not think we shall want again the word "buzz"—the name for the strange three-cornered chisel used for cleaning out the mortices of a stock and, to the best of my belief, used for nothing else, unless for enlarging the central hole in the stock.

And now—how dare I go on to describe that swinging drive of the wheelwright's action, fixing the spokes into the stock? Prose has no rhythm for it—no spring, no smashing blow recurrent at just the right time and place. The stock is to be imagined, ready at last, clamped down across the wheel-pit. From the front of it the gauge slants up; the dozen or fourteen spokes are near at hand, each with its tenon or "foot" numbered (in scribbled pencilling) to match the number scribbled against its own place in the stock. For although uniformity has been aimed at throughout, still every mortice has been chiselled to receive its own special spoke, lest the latter should by chance have had any small splinter broken away after all. The true wheelwright would not take that chance. He intended that every spoke should really fit tight; and there he has the spokes all numbered, to his hand.

He picks up one in one hand, and, with sledge-hammer in the other, lightly taps the spoke into its own mortice. Then he steps back, glancing behind him belike to see that the coast is clear; and, testing the distance with another light tap (a two-handed tap this time) suddenly, with a leap, he swings the sledge round full circle with both hands, and brings it down right on the top of the spoke—bang. Another blow or so, and the spoke is far enough into the mortice to be gauged. Is it leaning forward a little too much, or not quite enough? It can be corrected, with batterings properly planted on front or back of top, and accordingly the wheelwright aims his sledge, swinging it round tremendously again and again, until the spoke is indeed "driven" into the stock. It is battered over on the top, but the oak stands firm in the mortice, to stay for years.

For an hour or so, until all the spokes had been driven into a wheel, this sledge-hammer work went on, tremendous. I have seen nothing else like it. Road-menders greatly smite an iron wedge into the road they are breaking up; blacksmiths' mates use a ponderous sledge at some of their work; foresters, cleaving, make great play with beetle and wedges; but so far as I have noticed, these men (like the "Try-Your-Strength" men at a country fair) do not really know how to use sledge or beetle. They raise it up above their heads and bring it down, thump, with all the force of strong arms; but a wheelwright driving spokes, though not necessarily a very strong man, was able, with knack, to strike more powerful blows, and many of them too, in succession. With one hand close under the head he gave the sledge a great fling, then slipped the same hand down the handle, to help the other hand hold it in and guide it truly round its circle. By the time it reached the spoke the sledge had got an impetus. With the momentum of a stone from a sling, it was so to speak hurled down on its mark, terrific.

This way of driving spokes was probably very antique, and, being laborious and costly, it had died out from my shop before I had to retire myself. Hoop-tyres, superseding strakes, had indeed made such strenuous arm-work less necessary; and the lighter wheels for spring-vans and carts, besides being more rapidly worn out on the harder roads and at the quicker pace, did not otherwise need putting together so strongly. But a dung-cart or a wagon was meant to last a life-time: the wheels were heavy; "strakes" of old could not pull them together as more modern tyres did; the wheels might have to lie on their face in a meadow all the summer for "stepping" a rick-pole and then be put to their proper use again, and if they could not stand all this the wheelwright was sure to hear of it from the farmer.

So, in my first five or six years at my shop, Cook (and perhaps others) made wheels in the right provincial style—wheels to stand hard work until they fairly wore out. As I saw it practised the art must have been time-honoured indeed. Village shops had carried it on for generations. I like to think that the twelve-spoke wheel—the cart wheel—in one of the Canterbury Tales—was the work of men using the sledge as I saw George Cook using it.

II

George Cook, so often mentioned in these pages, was not a very singular man in his own time, but he was of a type almost forgotten nowadays. I recall nobody like him in any English book at all. What comes to my mind in thinking of Cook is a village flavour—the flavour preserved in some of the tales of Alsace in various Erckmann-Chatrian books. His attitude was that of a very efficient if very unsophisticated provincial, keeping close to the materials of his own neighbourhood and in touch with the personal crafts of his own people. The craft in which he himself specialized had made him rather round-shouldered; he was narrow chested too and a little inclined to bronchitis. By no means a large man, and slightly bandy-legged and slightly stooping, with toes tending to turn in, he moved nimbly—you couldn't call it exactly fast—always at one quite respectable pace. His sallow face had but a few thin hairs for beard and whiskers. His speech, so quiet, was just a trifle "blobby," as if he has something in his mouth, and to be sure he often was chewing a quid. The consequent spitting—anywhere and often—was not pleasant, but otherwise it was always agreeable to be where George Cook was. I never but once saw him angry—it was over some affair in his own family which he chose to confide to me—and even then he was not loud. I think his idea was to slip through life effective and inconspicuous, like a sharp-edged tool through hard wood. It was worth while to see him on a Sunday in most respectable black.

I don't know what he wore on weekdays. He took his breakfast and dinner at "The Seven Stars"; then, the day's work done, he went padding off home—it was a sort of jog-trot—to Compton. Being rather deaf, he never had a companion; but, away from the shop, he had a pipe. Smoking, it hardly needs saying, was not countenanced in the shop.

Of course my acquaintance with him was chiefly at work—at his bench or his chopping block, at the wheel-pit or the lathe or the timber stack. From the front edge of his bench a small point of steel stuck out about an eighth of an inch. Very bright it shone, because he pivoted his spokes tightly upon it when shaving them. The other end of the spoke was pressed against his waist. For this purpose he wore, strapped round him, a thick leather pad. I never knew anybody else have such a thing, but I suspect it was a part of a wheel-maker's outfit, and only partially effective. During my father's last illness a hard place on his waist, puzzling to the doctor, was explained as due to spoke-shaving, but perhaps he used no pad. In later years Cook adopted some revolving clamps for this purpose.

He was a left-handed man. Other workmen might be annoyed by apprentices or ignorant boys using their sharp axes; but you didn't do that twice with George Cook's axe—it was too dangerous a trick. Why did the confounded tool, albeit so keen-edged, seem to avoid the hard wood and aim viciously towards your thigh, or try to chop your fingers off? The reason was that in making the "shaft" for it (every good wheel-wright put the ash shaft or handle to his own axe)

Cook gave to his a slight bias for the left hand instead
of for the right. The blade too was ground on the
unaccustomed side. And though you might not have
noticed these peculiarities before, you soon were scared
into learning something about them if you foolishly
tried to use the axe. Cook smiled. Besides his axe, of
course he put in the shaft for his adze and handles for
his hammers. He made his own mallets and gauges,
and the "pegs" for his chisels. Truly it would not have
been easy to put him out with an edged tool. I have
seen him filing a sharper "nose" to an auger. It needed
a sharp auger for some of his work. When he was
boring inch-and-a-quarter holes in a set of dung cart
felloes the sweat would pour in streams from his pale
face; but he used to look round with a deprecating
smile, as who should say, "I'm sorry, but it can't be
helped." He had a little grease-box—that too hand-
made—hanging amongst the row of chisels over his
bench. But, come to think of it, every bench had this.
A big auger-hole in a shaped-out block of tough beech
served the purpose admirably. You could thrust your
finger (I wonder why I preferred the middle finger?)
into the grease-pot close at hand and easily take out
grease for anointing both sides of your saw or the face
of your plane.

Cook was, as I have said, deaf, and if you wanted to
attract his attention when his back was turned it was
useless to call to him. The best plan was to toss a little
chip either to touch him or to arrest his sight. I laughed
to myself once to see him and Will Hammond—far
more deaf even than Cook—searching for something
in a heap of felloe-patterns. Probably the blacksmith

wanted a pattern for strakes. At any rate it was odd to see these two with their heads together making some sort of friendly conversation by involuntary signs, since neither could have heard the other's mutterings. When Cook wanted a felloe-pattern for himself, he did not hunt long for a ready-made one. It was easier to him to strike out a new one that should be exactly what he required. But it must be said that no mere pattern, newly made out of thin board, equalled the felloes he afterwards got out in accordance with it. When he had finished with a felloe, the belly of it (the inner curve) hewn out with his adze, was as smooth, to the exact dimensions too, as if it had been polished.

So much for his skill as a craftsman. But when he got home he became, rather, a villager, accomplished in genial rustic arts. The hamlet of Compton was a little nook of heath and scrubby oaks, tucked away warm and secluded between Culverlands and Waverley woods, an outlying end, I think, of Farnham Common. No high-road even now has found it. You get to it by narrow tracks of carts up and down bosky hillocks, and I fancy the place is less populous to-day than it was forty years ago—which isn't saying much. It was probably a haunt of squatters, like its more out-at-elbows neighbour, The Bourne (Bettesworth's home), a mile away. Here dwelt Cook with his big family, in a little brick cottage, his mother (a widow then) living with him. Probably she was the owner of the cottage, and of the tiny hop-kiln adjoining it.

The hop-kiln, when I saw it, chiefly interested me as the quiet scene of George Cook's annual labours. Every autumn, namely in September, he used to tell me he

should be away from the shop for about a week, drying
his (or perhaps he said his mother's) hops. I wondered
chiefly at his having the staying power to do this—for
it was an unsleeping sort of job. Seeing it was Cook I
did not so much wonder at his ability; yet it was by no
means every working man in Farnham who had the
sense—the judgment—to dry hops, even when the
hop trade was at its best and everybody looked upon a
good dryer with a sort of friendly admiration. George
Cook's turn at it was probably a holiday for him. I like
to think of him in that little quiet kiln with the pungent
scent of the hops all about him—their golden dust
looking like the September sunshine grown solid. To
be there at home, with your pipe whenever you
wanted, and no wearisome walking—it was a pleasant
change from making wheels to order. Here, in the kiln,
a man was his own master. The hops alone had any
claim on him. If his arduous duty to them would allow
—and Cook would enjoy it the better for its being
arduous—he might trot up the ladder to the upper
floor whenever he liked; and there, with the sleepy-
scented hops on the floor behind him, he could stand
at the open doorway and see over the little hamlet—
the tiny hop-ground, his garden, the autumn woods—
could watch the neighbours and his own family down
there in the pleasant light, and feel himself a man of
importance amongst them, forgetting his daily wage-
earning. An acceptable break in his long year's work
this week must have made for him.

Of his garden I remember nothing. But I can surmise that the seasonal interests of it were his all the year
round. Did he keep a pig, I wonder? That there was a

donkey—of course with stable, hay, and all manner of country accessories—I do happen to know, for his mother's donkey-cart was sometimes mended in the old shop.

But of all his country crafts the most real part to me was the making of elderberry wine. I surmised his gardening and his keeping of donkey and pigs; I heard of his hop-drying; but of the elderberry wine I had personal knowledge.

It was like this. One winter Cook was ill for weeks with some eye trouble that would not yield to the treatment of the club doctor and in the end had to be treated at Moorfields Hospital. During that time I used to go to his cottage about once a week to make enquiries. This was after work was done. The walk out of Farnham up the hill into the night, then down the steeper hill under the pitchy darkness of Culverlands trees into the all but unknown murk of Compton— this mile and a half or so which was Cook's daily portion when he was in health—found its goal when at last the cottage door was opened and, momentarily dazzled, I was let in from the night to the little warm-lit living-room. Of all this, however, little or no recollection remains. Save for the light I cannot recover any memory of the room or its inmates. I only remember that I was expected to drink, and therefore did drink, about three parts of a tumblerful of hot elderberry wine. It was "the thing" to do for keeping out the cold, and it did keep out the cold. The Cooks evidently looked upon it as the natural reward after my walk and a proper preparation for the return. Two or three times this must have happened, and I surmise that the winter nights were cold as well as dark—that the ruts in the road were frozen hard under one's feet, and so on. But the point now is this elderberry wine. It gives a provincial air. Anything less suggestive of the London suburbs can hardly be imagined. It means that the Cooks knew how to live in a country hamlet. Where a city dweller would be helpless this family profited by centuries of tradition, and they were keeping old England going ("old" England, not modern England) when they made their elderberry wine and warmed some of it up for a friend on a cold winter night.

I cannot remember when Cook left Compton and came to live in Farnham. It seemed a good thing for him; good to be able to get to and from his work without that long hill. For the hilly walk used to set him coughing convulsively and for a long time, and during a fit of coughing the water would stream from his eyes. I was glad for him to be spared this exhaustion morning and night. Now, there were but three or four minutes of level street between his home and his work.

But who shall judge the cost of this change—from woodlands to the neighbourhood of gas-works, from old English rusticity to the state of the proletariat of the eighteen-nineties? I suppose that Cook's mother had died and that her little property had to be shared amongst her several sons and daughters; but anyhow it was a come-down for Cook, not financially only, when he had to leave Compton. I begin to think it was a come-down for me too, little though I dreamt of such a thing at the time. My intercourse with him underwent a profound though unnoticed change. Precisely where he got to in Farnham I never learnt. There was no need for me to go to see him. When at last, after many years, he took to his bed and died, I not only left him alone: I didn't even go to his funeral. It's true I was myself down with bronchitis at that time; but the fact remains —and I am not proud of it—that I had unawares allowed a gulf to widen between George Cook and myself.

I did not know it at the time. I always chatted with him for a minute or two every day. I never failed to sympathize with his winter desire for the return of cuckoo-time, or to laugh at his assumed dismalness (so characteristic of an ageing villager) before any cheerful prospect. Thus if, in mid December, I happened to remark " We shall soon have Christmas here," then he, assenting, was sure to add gloomily, " Whoever lives to see it!" whereat we smiled as if we liked one another. Yet, for all this, we were no longer on the old terms. I was not in touch, through him, with the quiet dignified country life of England and I was more of a capitalist. Each of us had slipped a little nearer to the ignominious class division of these present times—I to the employer's side, he to the disregarded workman's. The mutual respect was decaying. Nor yet might Cook, for his part, view his own life with the earlier satisfaction. From being one of a community of rustics, he was becoming more and more a mechanic—a cog in an industrial machine. Those were not yet the days of " Unrest." The stealthy changes which were destined, after thirty years, to oust the old skill altogether seemed to Cook, if he discerned them at all, due to his advancing years. If life was meaner, less interesting, than of old, was it not chiefly because he had been born too

soon? He would have said so. He remained an opinion-
ated Conservative and read *The Standard* every day.

From "The Wheelwright's Shop"

---

*Sturt found writing difficult and slow; he set about it, as
about fashioning a tool for use, with proper patience and
care and sense of purpose. He has to convey a sense of a
cultural inheritance; he has to convey what lies near the
heart of the vocation to good workmanship. His prose
fashions itself in a way to embody these things: it is unhurried,
chaste, and free of all ornament or falsity; its idiom is near
to speech, but weighty, patient speech. Like the craftsman's
skill, it is dedicated to its purpose. No one has written
better in this kind; Sturt himself (originally under the
name George Bourne) wrote equally well in "The Bettesworth Book" and "Change in the Village" (Duckworth).
Behind such prose lie Cobbett's "Rural Rides" (Every-
man) and some of the finest work of Jefferies, like "The
Gamekeeper at Home," and "Hodge and his Masters"
(Faber and Faber). The writing there is not less crisp and
vigorous than Sturt's. Alongside comes such work as
Adrian Bell's "Corduroy" (Bodley Head) and the
books of Edward Thomas (whose prose appears later in
this collection).*

*Quite another tradition of dedication and craftsmanship
of obligation and honour appears in the opening sections
('Ordeal by Water' is their title) of the next book to be
represented here: Joseph Conrad's "The Mirror of the
Sea:" it may prove well worthwhile comparing the sailor's
vocation with the wheelwright's.*

IV

The Artist's Vision

Ordeal by Water
Joseph Conrad

Joseph Conrad is one of the great English novelists. In what follows, he brings the power of the imaginative artist to bear upon an episode in his own earlier experience as a man learning the sailor's craft; he gives to it a universal tone. The experience becomes a significant human experience, not just something that had happened to Conrad.

He was born of Polish landowners in 1857, and died, an English citizen, in Kent in 1924. He left his native land, then under Russian tyranny, to become a sailor. At twenty he was gun-running for Spanish Royalists. At twenty-five he had sailed East and West. At twenty-nine he had learned our language, mastered our technical manuals, and become a Master Mariner in the Merchant Service. At thirty-eight he had become a novelist and retired from the sea. To the skill of a story-teller, therefore, he added wide-ranging knowledge of seas, nations, and people, and a long, close intimacy with ships and sailors, and an incomparable store of memories. Both the sailor's and the novelist's callings were to him crafts as sacred as George Sturt's or Eric Gill's or Beatrice Webb's were to them. That we know from The Fine Art, earlier in this book. But the sailor has his business in great waters; he has to encounter dangers and trials quite remote from theirs. Of these, this prose speaks; the theme with which it opens must by now sound very familiar.

THE love that is given to ships is profoundly different from the love men feel for every other work
of their hands—the love they bear to their houses, for
instance—because it is untainted by the pride of possession. The pride of skill, the pride of responsibility,
the pride of endurance there may be, but otherwise it
is a disinterested sentiment. No seaman ever cherished
a ship, even if she belonged to him, merely because of
the profit she put in his pocket. No one I think, ever
did; for a ship-owner, even of the best, has always been
outside the pale of that sentiment embracing in a feeling of intimate, equal fellowship the ship and the man,
backing each other against the implacable, if sometimes dissembled, hostility of their world of waters.
The sea—this truth must be confessed—has no generosity. No display of manly qualities—courage, hardihood, endurance, faithfulness—has ever been known
to touch its irresponsible consciousness of power. The
ocean has the conscienceless temper of a savage auto-
crat spoiled by much adulation. He cannot brook the
slightest appearance of defiance, and has remained the
irreconcilable enemy of ships and men ever since ships
and men had the unheard-of audacity to go afloat
together in the face of his frown. From that day he has
gone on swallowing up fleets and men without his
resentment being glutted by the number of victims—
by so many wrecked ships and wrecked lives. To-day,
as ever, he is ready to beguile and betray, to smash and
to drown the incorrigible optimism of men who,
backed by the fidelity of ships, are trying to wrest from

him the fortune of their house, the dominion of their world, or only a dole of food for their hunger. If not always in the hot mood to smash, he is always stealthily ready for a drowning. The most amazing wonder of the deep is its unfathomable cruelty.

I felt its dread for the first time in mid-Atlantic one day, many years ago, when we took off the crew of a Danish brig homeward bound from the West Indies. A thin, silvery mist softened the calm and majestic splendour of light without shadows—seemed to render the sky less remote and the ocean less immense. It was one of the days, when the might of the sea appears indeed lovable, like the nature of a strong man in moments of quiet intimacy. At sunrise we had made out a black speck to the westward, apparently suspended high up in the void behind a stirring, shimmering veil of silvery blue gauze that seemed at times to stir and float in the breeze which fanned us slowly along. The peace of that enchanting forenoon was so profound, so untroubled, that it seemed that every word pronounced loudly on our deck would penetrate to the very heart of that infinite mystery born from the conjunction of water and sky. We did not raise our voices. "A water-logged derelict, I think, sir," said the second officer, quietly, coming down from aloft with the binoculars in their case slung across his shoulders; and our captain, without a word, signed to the helmsman to steer for the black speck. Presently we made out a low, jagged stump sticking up forward—all that remained of her departed masts.

The captain was expatiating in a low conversational tone to the chief mate upon the danger of these derelicts, and upon his dread of coming upon them at night, when suddenly a man forward screamed out, "There's people on board of her, sir! I see them!" in a most extraordinary voice—a voice never heard before in our ship; the amazing voice of a stranger. It gave the signal for a sudden tumult of shouts. The watch below ran up the forecastle head in a body, the cook dashed out of the galley. Everybody saw the poor fellows now. They were there! And all at once our ship, which had the well-earned name of being without a rival for speed in light winds, seemed to us to have lost power of motion, as if the sea, becoming viscous, had clung to her sides. And yet she moved. Immensity, the inseparable companion of a ship's life, chose that day to breathe upon her as gently as a sleeping child. The clamour of our excitement had died out, and our living ship, famous for never losing steerage way as long as there was air enough to float a feather, stole, without a ripple, silent and white as a ghost, towards her mutilated and wounded sister, come upon at the point of death in the sunlit haze of a calm day at sea.

With the binoculars glued to his eyes, the captain said in a quavering tone: "They are waving to us with something aft there." He put down the glasses on the skylight brusquely, and began to walk about the poop. "A shirt or a flag," he ejaculated, irritably. "Can't make it out. . . . Some damn rag or other!" He took a few more turns on the poop, glancing down over the rail now and then to see how fast we were moving. His nervous footsteps rang sharply in the quiet of the ship, where the other men, all looking the same way, had forgotten themselves in a staring immobility.

"This will never do!" he cried out, suddenly. "Lower the boats at once! Down with them!"

Before I jumped into mine he took me aside, as being an experienced junior, for a word of warning:

"You look out as you come alongside that she doesn't take you down with her. You understand?"

He murmured this confidentially, so that none of the men at the falls should overhear, and I was shocked. "Heavens! as if in such an emergency one stopped to think of danger!" I exclaimed to myself mentally, in scorn of such cold-blooded caution.

It takes many lessons to make a real seaman, and I got my rebuke at once. My experienced commander seemed in one searching glance to read my thoughts on my ingenuous face.

"What you're going for is to save life, not to drown your boat's crew for nothing," he growled severely, in my ear. But as we shoved off he leaned over and cried out: "It all rests on the power of your arms, men. Give way for life!"

We made a race of it, and I would never have believed that a common boat's crew of a merchantman could keep up so much determined fierceness in the regular swing of their stroke. What our captain had clearly perceived before we left had become plain to all of us since. The issue of our enterprise hung on a hair above that abyss of waters which will not give up its dead till the Day of Judgment. It was a race of two ship's boats matched against Death for a prize of nine men's lives, and Death had a long start. We saw the crew of the brig from afar working at the pumps— still pumping on that wreck, which already had settled so far down that the gentle, low swell, over which our boats rose and fell easily without a check to their speed, welling up almost level with her headrails, plucked at the ends of broken gear swinging desolately under her naked bowsprit.

We could not, in all conscience, have picked out a better day for our regatta had we had the free choice of all the days that ever dawned upon the lonely struggles and solitary agonies of ships since the Norse rovers first steered to the westward against the run of Atlantic waves. It was a very good race. At the finish there was not an oar's length between the first and second boat, with Death coming in a good third on the top of the very next smooth swell, for all one knew to the contrary. The scuppers of the brig gurgled softly all together when the water rising against her sides subsided sleepily with a low wash, as if playing about an immovable rock. Her bulwarks were gone fore and aft, and one saw her bare deck low-lying like a raft and swept clean of boats, spars, houses—of everything except the ringbolts and the heads of the pumps. I had one dismal glimpse of it as I braced myself up to receive upon my breast the last man to leave her, the captain, who literally let himself fall into my arms.

It had been a weirdly silent rescue—a rescue without a hail, without a single uttered word, without a gesture or a sign, without a conscious exchange of glances. Up to the very last moment those on board stuck to their pumps, which spouted two clear streams of water upon their bare feet. Their brown skin showed through the rents of their shirts; and the two small bunches of half-naked, tattered men went on bowing from the waist to each other in their back-breaking labour, up and down, absorbed, with no time for a glance over the shoulder at the help that was coming to them. As we dashed, unregarded, alongside a voice let out one, only one hoarse howl of command, and then, just as they stood, without caps, with the salt drying grey in the wrinkles and folds of their hairy, haggard faces, blinking stupidly at us their red eyelids, they made a bolt away from the handles, tottering and jostling against each other, and positively flung themselves over upon our very heads. The clatter they made tumbling into the boats had an extraordinarily destructive effect upon the illusion of tragic dignity our self-esteem had thrown over the contests of mankind with the sea. On that exquisite day of gentle breathing peace and veiled sunshine perished my romantic love to what men's imagination had proclaimed the most august aspect of Nature. The cynical indifference of the sea to the merits of human suffering and courage, laid bare in this ridiculous, panic-tainted performance extorted from the dire extremity of nine good and honourable seamen revolted me. I saw the duplicity of the sea's most tender mood. It was so because it could not help itself but the awed respect of the early days was gone. I felt ready to smile bitterly at its enchanting charm and glare viciously at its furies. In a moment, before we shoved off, I had looked coolly at the life of my choice. Its illusions were gone, but its fascination remained. I had become a seaman at last.

We pulled hard for a quarter of an hour, then laid on our oars waiting for our ship. She was coming down on us with swelling sails, looking delicately tall and exquisitely noble through the mist. The captain of the brig, who sat in the stern sheets by my side with his face in his hands, raised his head and began to speak with a sort of sombre volubility. They had lost their masts and sprung a leak in a hurricane; drifted for weeks, always at the pumps, met more bad weather; the ships they sighted failed to make them out, the leak gained upon them slowly, and the seas had left them nothing to make a raft of. It was very hard to see ship after ship pass by at a distance, "as if everybody had agreed that we must be left to drown," he added. But they went on trying to keep the brig afloat as long as possible, and working the pumps constantly on insufficient food, mostly raw, till "yesterday evening," he continued, monotonously, "just as the sun went down, the men's hearts broke."

He made an almost imperceptible pause here, and went on again with exactly the same intonation:

"They told me the brig could not be saved, and they thought they had done enough for themselves. I said nothing to that. It was true. It was no mutiny. I had nothing to say to them. They lay about aft all night, as still as so many dead men. I did not lie down. I kept a look-out. When the first light came I saw your ship at once. I waited for more light; the breeze began to fall on my face. Then I shouted out as loud as I was able, 'Look at that ship!' but only two men got up very slowly and came to me. At first only we three stood alone, for a long time, watching you coming down to us, and feeling the breeze drop to a calm almost; but afterwards others, too, rose, one after another, and by and by I had all my crew behind me.

I turned round and said to them that they could see the ship was coming our way, but in this small breeze she might come too late after all, unless we turned to and tried to keep the brig afloat long enough to give you time to save us all. I spoke like that to them, and then I gave the command to man the pumps."

He gave the command, and gave the example, too, by going himself to the handles, but it seems that these men did actually hang back for a moment, looking at each other dubiously before they followed him. "He! he! he!" He broke out into a most unexpected, imbecile, pathetic, nervous little giggle. "Their hearts were broken so! They had been played with too long," he explained, apologetically, lowering his eyes, and became silent.

Twenty-five years is a long time—a quarter of a century is a dim and distant past; but to this day I remember the dark-brown feet, hands, and faces of two of these men whose hearts had been broken by the sea. They were lying very still on their sides on the bottom boards between the thwarts, curled up like dogs. My boat's crew, leaning over the looms of their oars, stared and listened as if at the play. The master of the brig looked up suddenly to ask me what day it was.

They had lost the date. When I told him it was Sunday, the 22nd, he frowned, making some mental calculation, then nodded twice sadly to himself, staring at nothing.

His aspect was miserably unkempt and wildly sorrowful. Had it not been for the unquenchable candour of his blue eyes, whose unhappy, tired glance every moment sought his abandoned, sinking brig, as if it

could find rest nowhere else, he would have appeared
mad. But he was too simple to go mad, too simple with
that manly simplicity which alone can bear men un-
scathed in mind and body through an encounter with
the deadly playfulness of the sea or with its less
abominable fury.

Neither angry, nor playful, nor smiling, it enveloped
our distant ship growing bigger as she neared us, our
boats with the rescued men and the dismantled hull of
the brig we were leaving behind, in the large and
placid embrace of its quietness, half lost in the fair haze,
as if in a dream of infinite and tender clemency. There
was no frown, no wrinkle on its face, not a ripple. And
the run of the slight swell was so smooth that it
resembled the graceful undulation of a piece of shimmering grey silk shot with gleams of green. We pulled
an easy stroke; but when the master of the brig, after
a glance over his shoulder, stood up with a low exclamation, my men feathered their oars instinctively,
without an order, and the boat lost her way.

He was steadying himself on my shoulders with a
strong grip, while his other arm, flung up rigidly,
pointed a denunciatory finger at the immense tran-
quillity of the ocean. After his first exclamation, which
stopped the swing of our oars, he made no sound, but
his whole attitude seemed to cry out an indignant
"Behold!" . . . I could not imagine what vision of
evil had come to him. I was startled, and the amazing
energy of his immobilized gesture made my heart beat
faster with the anticipation of something monstrous
and unsuspected. The stillness around us became
crushing.

For a moment the succession of silky undulations ran on innocently. I saw each of them swell up the misty line of the horizon, far, far away beyond the derelict brig, and the next moment, with a slight friendly toss of our boat, it had passed under us and was gone. The lulling cadence of the rise and fall, the invariable gentleness of this irresistible force, the great charm of the deep waters, warmed my breast deliciously, like the subtle poison of a love-potion. But all this lasted only a few soothing seconds before I jumped up, too, making the boat roll like the veriest land-lubber.

Something startling, mysterious, hastily confused was taking place. I watched it with incredulous and fascinated awe, as one watches the confused, swift movements of some deed of violence done in the dark. As if at a given signal, the run of the smooth undulations seemed checked suddenly around the brig. By a strange optical delusion the whole sea appeared to rise upon her in one overwhelming heave of its silky surface where in one spot a smother of foam broke out ferociously. And then the effort subsided. It was all over, and the smooth swell ran on as before from the horizon in uninterrupted cadence of motion, passing under us with a slight friendly toss of our boat. Far away, where the brig had been, an angry white stain undulating on the surface of steely-grey waters, shot with gleams of green, diminished swiftly without a hiss, like a patch of pure snow melting in the sun. And the great stillness after this initiation into the sea's implacable hate seemed full of dread thoughts and shadows of disaster.

"Gone!" ejaculated from the depths of his chest my bowman in a final tone. He spat in his hands, and took a better grip on his oar. The captain of the brig lowered his rigid arm slowly, and looked at our faces in a solemnly conscious silence, which called upon us to share in his simple-minded, marvelling awe. All at once he sat down by my side, and leaned forward earnestly at my boat's crew, who, swinging together in a long, easy stroke, kept their eyes fixed upon him faithfully.

"No ship could have done so well," he addressed them, firmly, after a moment of strained silence, during which he seemed with trembling lips to seek for words fit to bear such high testimony. "She was small, but she was good. I had no anxiety. She was strong. Last voyage I had my wife and two children in her. No other ship could have stood so long the weather she had to live through for days and days before we got dismasted a fortnight ago. She was fairly worn out, and that's all. You may believe me. She lasted under us for days and days, but she could not last for ever. It was long enough. I am glad it is over. No better ship was ever left to sink at sea on such a day as this."

He was competent to pronounce the funeral oration of a ship, this son of ancient sea-folk, whose national existence, so little stained by the excesses of manly virtues, had demanded nothing but the merest foot-hold from the earth. By the merits of his sea-wise fore-fathers and by the artlessness of his heart, he was made fit to deliver this excellent discourse. There was nothing wanting in its orderly arrangement—neither piety nor faith, nor the tribute of praise due to the

worthy dead, with the edifying recital of their achievement. She had lived, he had loved her; she had suffered,
and he was glad she was at rest. It was an excellent
discourse. And it was orthodox, too, in its fidelity to
the cardinal article of a seaman's faith, of which it was
a single-minded confession. "Ships are all right." They
are. They who live with the sea have got to hold by
that creed first and last; and it came to me, as I glanced
at him sideways, that some men were not altogether
unworthy in honour and conscience to pronounce the
funeral eulogium of a ship's constancy in life and death.

After this, sitting by my side with his loosely clasped
hands hanging between his knees, he uttered no word,
made no movement, till the shadow of our ship's sails
fell on the boat, when, at the loud cheer greeting the
return of the victors with their prize, he lifted up his
troubled face with a faint smile of pathetic indulgence.
This smile of the worthy descendant of the most
ancient sea-folk, whose audacity and hardihood had
left no trace of greatness and glory upon the waters,
completed the cycle of my initiation. There was an
infinite depth of hereditary wisdom in its pitying sadness. It made the hearty bursts of cheering sound like
a childish noise of triumph. Our crew shouted with
immense confidence—honest souls! As if anybody
could ever make sure of having prevailed against the
sea, which has betrayed so many ships of great "name,"
so many proud men, so many towering ambitions of
fame, power, wealth, greatness!

As I brought the boat under the falls my captain, in
high good-humour, leaned over, spreading his red and
freckled elbows on the rail, and called down to me

sarcastically out of the depths of his cynic philosopher's beard:

"So you have brought the boat back after all, have you?"

Sarcasm was "his way," and the most that can be said for it is that it was natural. This did not make it lovable. But it is decorous and expedient to fall in with one's commander's way. "Yes. I brought the boat back all right, Sir," I answered. And the good man believed me. It was not for him to discern upon me the marks of my recent initiation. And yet I was not exactly the same youngster who had taken the boat away —all impatience for a race against Death, with the prize of nine men's lives at the end.

Already I looked with other eyes upon the sea. I knew it capable of betraying the generous ardour of youth as implacably as, indifferent to evil and good, it would have betrayed the basest greed or the noblest heroism. My conception of its magnanimous greatness was gone. And I looked upon the true sea—the sea that plays with men till their hearts are broken, and wears stout ships to death. Nothing can touch the brooding bitterness of its soul. Open to all and faithful to none, it exercises its fascination for the undoing of the best. To love it is not well. It knows no bond of plighted troth, no fidelity to misfortune, to long companionship, to long devotion. The promise it holds out perpetually is very great; but the only secret of its possession is strength, strength—the jealous, sleepless strength of a man guarding a coveted treasure within his gates.

From " The Mirror of the Sea"

There is eloquence, richly sensuous description, impassioned feeling; at the same time there is subtle observation (the sailor's trained eye misses little); and a motion of tough humour; and a free, darting play of the mental and spiritual powers. The experience was personal and actual; but prose like this turns the imaginative insight of the twenty-five years since upon it, and holds it up to that light. So the reader has also to live through an initiation, has to be made free of a realm of danger, and to understand deep issues.

In sensuous power and natural eloquence there is no prose superior to the best of Conrad's. The last two readings in this book will usefully compare with it, but cannot surpass it. And although as a novelist Conrad has subjects profounder than 'sea stories' would suggest, it is the sea whose character and appearances he has most uniquely found a prose for. The wonderful stories "Typhoon," "The Nigger of the Narcissus," and "The Shadow Line" (Dent) witness to that. Yet the African Congo (in "Heart of Darkness") and the dingy London shop (in "The Secret Agent") reveal an equal power.

Joseph Conrad
Virginia Woolf

Here is the tribute Virginia Woolf paid to Conrad when he died in 1924. (Thomas Hardy was still living; he is the obvious exception referred to in the essay.) It is not a critical verdict: the time was not ripe for that. It has the generosity of a tribute, but it also marks a stock-taking of the kind to which the death of a great master stirs one. Virginia Woolf was herself a novelist, a fellow-craftsman with Conrad; but though a very original one, she had her roots in a world far narrower than his. He was, in more than the literal sense of the opening paragraph, a stranger.

She was born in London in 1882, the daughter of a dis-tinguished philosopher and critic, Leslie Stephen. She died in 1941, in Sussex. She became not only a novelist of rare gifts, but also an important member of that group of writers, artists, and intellectuals who drew out of the Cambridge society already referred to, and first gathered at her house in Bloomsbury. They believed in the supreme importance of art in the modern world; in the love of beautiful things, and in personal affection, as the highest goods. They were gay, fastidious, urbane, superior, sceptical: they stiffened, with mutual admiration and with reliance upon one another's judgments, their position of proud hostility to the uncultured world about them.

Virginia Woolf was of them, as E. M. Forster was; but both had a tough and independent core to their spirits. At such a moment as the death of Conrad, and the

*urgent commission of " The Times Literary Supplement"
to say something adequate about him, Virginia Woolf
became very much more than the member of a restricted
London group. A deeper note sounds.*

SUDDENLY, without giving us time to arrange our
thoughts or prepare our phrases, our guest has left
us; and his withdrawal without farewell or ceremony
is in keeping with his mysterious arrival, long years
ago, to take up his lodging in this country. For there
was always an air of mystery about him. It was partly
his Polish birth, partly his memorable appearance,
partly his preference for living in the depths of the
country, out of ear-shot of gossips, beyond reach of
hostesses, so that for news of him one had to depend
upon the evidence of simple visitors with a habit of
ringing doorbells who reported of their unknown host
that he had the most perfect manners, the brightest
eyes, and spoke English with a strong foreign accent.

Still, though it is the habit of death to quicken and
focus our memories, there clings to the genius of
Conrad something essentially, and not accidentally,
difficult of approach. His reputation of later years was,
with one obvious exception, undoubtedly the highest
in England; yet he was not popular. He was read with
passionate delight by some; others he left cold and
lustreless. Among his readers were people of the most
opposite ages and sympathies. Schoolboys of fourteen,
driving their way through Marryat, Scott, Henty, and
Dickens swallowed him down with the rest; while the
seasoned and the fastidious, who in process of time

have eaten their way to the heart of literature and there
turn over and over a few precious crumbs, set Conrad
scrupulously upon their banqueting table. One source
of difficulty and disagreement is, of course, to be found
where men have at all times found it, in his beauty.
One opens his pages and feels as Helen must have felt
when she looked in her glass and realized that, do what
she would, she could never in any circumstances pass
for a plain woman. So Conrad had been gifted, so he
had schooled himself, and such was his obligation to a
strange language wooed characteristically for its Latin
qualities rather than its Saxon, that it seemed impossible for him to make an ugly or insignificant movement of the pen. His mistress, his style, is a little
somnolent sometimes in repose. But let somebody
speak to her, and then how magnificently she bears
down upon us, with what colour, triumph, and
majesty! Yet it is arguable that Conrad would have
gained both in credit and in popularity if he had
written what he had to write without this incessant
care for appearances. They block and impede and dis-
tract, his critics say, pointing to those famous passages
which it is becoming the habit to lift from their con-
text and exhibit among other cut flowers of English
prose. He was self-conscious and stiff and ornate, they
complain, and the sound of his own voice was dearer
to him than the voice of humanity in its anguish. The
criticism is familiar, and as difficult to refute as the
remarks of deaf people when *Figaro* is played. They see
the orchestra; far off they hear a dismal scrape of sound;
their own remarks are interrupted, and, very naturally,
they conclude that the ends of life would be better

served if instead of scraping Mozart those fifty fiddlers broke stones upon the road. That beauty teaches, that beauty is a disciplinarian, how are we to convince them, since her teaching is inseparable from the sound of her voice and to that they are deaf? But read Conrad, not in birthday books but in the bulk, and he must be lost indeed to the meaning of words who does not hear in that rather stiff and sombre music, with its reserve, its pride, its vast and implacable integrity, how it is better to be good than bad, how loyalty is good and honesty and courage, though ostensibly Conrad is concerned merely to show us the beauty of a night at sea. But it is ill work dragging such intimations from their element. Dried in our little saucers, without the magic and mystery of language, they lose their power to excite and goad; they lose the drastic power which is a constant quality of Conrad's prose.

For it was by virtue of something drastic in him, the qualities of a leader and captain, that Conrad kept his hold over boys and young people. Until *Nostromo* was written his characters, as the young were quick to perceive, were fundamentally simple and heroic, however subtle the mind and indirect the method of their creator. They were seafarers, used to solitude and silence. They were in conflict with Nature, but at peace with man. Nature was their antagonist; she it was who drew forth honour, magnanimity, loyalty, the qualities proper to man; she who in sheltered bays reared to womanhood beautiful girls unfathomable and austere. Above all, it was Nature who turned out such gnarled and tested characters as Captain Whalley and old Singleton, obscure but glorious in their obscurity,

who were to Conrad the pick of our race, the men
whose praises he was never tired of celebrating:

They had been strong as those are strong who know
neither doubts nor hopes. They had been impatient and
enduring, turbulent and devoted, unruly and faithful.
Well-meaning people had tried to represent these men
as whining over every mouthful of their food, as going
about their work in fear of their lives. But in truth
they had been men who knew toil, privation, violence,
debauchery—but knew not fear, and had no desire of
spite in their hearts. Men hard to manage, but easy to
inspire; voiceless men—but men enough to scorn in
their hearts the sentimental voices that bewailed the
hardness of their fate. It was a fate unique and their
own; the capacity to bear it appeared to them the
privilege of the chosen! Their generation lived inarti-
culate and indispensable, without knowing the sweetness of affections or the refuge of a home—and died
free from the dark menace of a narrow grave. They
were the everlasting children of the mysterious sea.

Such were the characters of the early books—*Lord
Jim, Typhoon, The Nigger of the "Narcissus," Youth*; and
these books, in spite of the changes and fashions, are
surely secure of their place among our classics. But
they reach this height by means of qualities which the
simple story of adventure, as Marryat told it, or Feni-
more Cooper, has no claim to possess. For it is clear
that to admire and celebrate such men and such deeds,
romantically, whole-heartedly and with the fervour of
a lover, one must be possessed of the double vision;
one must be at once inside and out. To praise their
silence one must possess a voice. To appreciate their
endurance one must be sensitive to fatigue. One must

be able to live on equal terms with the Whalleys and
the Singletons and yet hide from their suspicious eyes
the very qualities which enable one to understand them.
Conrad alone was able to live that double life, for
Conrad was compound of two men; together with the
sea captain dwelt that subtle, refined, and fastidious
analyst whom he called Marlow. "A most discreet,
understanding man," he said of Marlow.

Marlow was one of those born observers who are
happiest in retirement. Marlow liked nothing better
than to sit on deck, in some obscure creek of the
Thames, smoking and recollecting; smoking and speculating; sending after his smoke beautiful rings of words
until all the summer's night became a little clouded
with tobacco smoke. Marlow, too, had a profound
respect for the men with whom he had sailed; but he
saw the humour of them. He nosed out and described
in masterly fashion those live creatures who prey
successfully upon the clumsy veterans. He had a flair
for human deformity; his humour was sardonic. Nor
did Marlow live entirely wreathed in the smoke of his
own cigars. He had a habit of opening his eyes suddenly and looking—at a rubbish heap, at a port, at a
shop counter—and then complete in its burning ring
of light that thing is flashed bright upon the mysterious
background. Introspective and analytical, Marlow was
aware of this peculiarity. He said the power came to
him suddenly. He might, for instance, overhear a
French officer murmur "Mon Dieu, how the time
passes!"

Nothing could have been more commonplace than
this remark; but its utterance coincided for me with a

moment of vision. It's extraordinary how we go
through life with eyes half shut, with dull ears, with
dormant thoughts. . . . Nevertheless, there can be but
few of us who had never known one of these rare
moments of awakening, when we see, hear, understand,
ever so much—everything—in a flash, before we fall
back again into our agreeable somnolence. I raised my
eyes when he spoke, and I saw him as though I had
never seen him before.

Picture after picture he painted thus upon that dark
background; ships first and foremost, ships at anchor,
ships flying before the storm, ships in harbour; he
painted sunsets and dawns; he painted the night; he
painted the sea in every aspect; he painted the gaudy
brilliancy of Eastern ports, and men and women, their
houses and their attitudes. He was an accurate and un-
flinching observer, schooled to that "absolute loyalty
towards his feelings and sensations," which, Conrad
wrote, "an author should keep hold of in his most
exalted moments of creation." And very quietly and
compassionately Marlow sometimes lets fall a few
words of epitaph which remind us, with all that beauty
and brilliancy before our eyes, of the darkness of the
background.

Thus a rough-and-ready distinction would make us
say that it is Marlow who comments, Conrad who
creates. It would lead us, aware that we are on dangerous ground to account for that change which,
Conrad tells us, took place when he had finished the
last story in the *Typhoon* volume—"a subtle change in
the nature of the inspiration" by some alteration in the
relationship of the two old friends. ". . . it seemed

somehow that there was nothing more in the world to write about." It was Conrad, let us suppose, Conrad the creator, who said that, looking back with sorrowful satisfaction upon the stories he had told; feeling as he well might that he could never better the storm in *The Nigger of the "Narcissus,"* or render more faithful tribute to the qualities of British seamen than he had done already in *Youth* and *Lord Jim*. It was then that Marlow, the commentator, reminded him how, in the course of nature, one must grow old, sit smoking on deck, and give up seafaring. But, he reminded him, those strenuous years had deposited their memories; and he even went so far perhaps as to hint that, though the last word might have been said about Captain Whalley and his relation to the universe, there remained on shore a number of men and women whose relationships, though of a more personal kind, might be worth looking into. If we further suppose that there was a volume of Henry James on board and that Marlow gave his friend the book to take to bed with him, we may seek support in the fact that it was in 1905 that Conrad wrote a very fine essay upon that master.

For some years, then it was Marlow who was the dominant partner. *Nostromo, Chance, The Arrow of Gold* represent that stage of the alliance which some will continue to find the richest of all. The human heart is more intricate than the forest, they will say; it has its storms; it has its creatures of the night; and if as novelist you wish to test man in all his relationships, the proper antagonist is man; his ordeal is in society, not solitude. For them there will always be a peculiar

fascination in the books where the light of those brilliant eyes falls not only upon the waste of waters but
upon the heart in its perplexity. But it must be ad-
mitted that, if Marlow thus advised Conrad to shift
his angle of vision, the advice was bold. For the vision
of a novelist is both complex and specialized; complex,
because behind his characters and apart from them
must stand something stable to which he relates them;
specialized because since he is a single person with one
sensibility the aspects of life in which he can believe
with conviction are strictly limited. So delicate a
balance is easily disturbed. After the middle period
Conrad never again was able to bring his figures into
perfect relation with their background. He never
believed in his later, and more highly sophisticated
characters as he had believed in his early seamen.
When he had to indicate their relation to that other
unseen world of novelists, the world of values and
convictions, he was far less sure what those values
were. Then, over and over again, a single phrase, "He
steered with care," coming at the end of a storm
carried in it a whole morality. But in this more crowded
and complicated world such terse phrases became less
and less appropriate. Complex men and women of
many interests and relations would not submit to so
summary a judgement; or, if they did, much that was
important in them escaped the verdict. And yet it was
very necessary to Conrad's genius, with its luxuriant
and romantic power, to have some law by which its
creations could be tried. Essentially—such remained
his creed—this world of civilized and self-conscious
people is based upon "a few very simple ideas"; but

where, in the world of thoughts and personal relations, are we to find them? There are no masts in drawing-rooms; the typhoon does not test the worth of politicians and business men. Seeking and not finding such supports, the world of Conrad's later period has about it an involuntary obscurity, an inconclusiveness, almost a disillusionment which baffles and fatigues. We lay hold in the dusk only of the old nobilities and sonorities: fidelity, compassion, honour, service—beautiful always, but now a little wearily reiterated, as if times had changed. Perhaps it was Marlow who was at fault. His habit of mind was a trifle sedentary. He had sat upon deck too long; splendid in soliloquy, he was less apt in the give and take of conversation; and those "moments of vision" flashing and fading, do not serve as well as steady lamplight to illumine the ripple of life and its long, gradual years. Above all, perhaps, he did not take into account how, if Conrad was to create, it was essential first that he should believe.

Therefore, though we shall make expeditions into the later books and bring back wonderful trophies, large tracts of them will remain by most of us untrodden. It is the earlier books—*Youth, Lord Jim, Typhoon, The Nigger of the "Narcissus"*—that we shall read in their entirety. For when the question is asked, what of Conrad will survive and where in the ranks of novelists we are to place him, these books, with their air of telling us something very old and perfectly true, which had lain hidden but is now revealed, will come to mind and make such questions and comparisons seem a little futile. Complete and still, very chaste and very beautiful, they rise in the memory as, on these hot summer nights, in their slow and stately way first one star comes out and then another.

From " The Common Reader"

She has turned our minds to Conrad's greatness as an imaginative novelist, and also to the nature of his prose. At the same time her own prose acts with all the delicacy of a gauge, detecting, measuring. It is a prose of the most refined sensitiveness, adapted to catch and suggest what is elusive, or subtle, on the very edges of our experience. At her best she writes with breathtaking grace, ingenuity, and control of nuance. Notice how pointedly the phrases register her feeling and her insights. Not that we have here the last word about Conrad's novels; the critic stands too close, and her vision is affected both by her own purposes as a novelist and by her background. In 1924, at the moment of his death, sorting out impressions, trying to define an impression of grandeur, the earlier and simpler novels seemed the more important. " Typhoon" and " The Nigger" still seem the imperishable tales of her vision; but " Nostromo," " Under Western Eyes," and " Victory" have, thirty years later, even greater power. Yet there remains an inimitable, generous glow about this tribute; few, at that time, appreciated Conrad with more justice. And if some part of his power had not yet penetrated the formalities of her world, yet she measured very surely that insight into the recesses of the human heart (and not just the moods of the sea) that made his masterpieces possible.

Many other essays in " The Common Reader" (available as a Penguin book) will give equal pleasure, and some of Virginia Woolf's finest passages are to be found in the informality of her " Diary" (Hogarth Press). But above all, to savour the fineness and originality of her prose one must go to her novels, " To the Lighthouse" in particular.

V

The Scientist's Vision

Charles Sherrington : *Man on His Nature*

William Bragg : *Concerning the Nature of Things*

The Miracle of the Human Eye
Charles Sherrington

We turn from the report the artist brings back from imaginative exploration of experience, to the report the scientist brings back from research, observation, measurement, information, deduction, and perception. Sir Charles Sherrington was born in 1857 and died in 1952. He was the chief pioneer of the experimental analysis of the central nervous system. His book, " The Integrative Action of the Nervous System," is among the classics of physiology and medical science. The description of the eye that follows comes from " Man on his Nature" (available as a Pelican book). This exposition of a biologist's philosophy and of the knowledge and observation upon which it is founded, Sherrington first gave in the form of lectures for the Gifford Foundation at Glasgow.

We saw something of the vocation of learning in E. M. Forster's account of Lowes Dickinson. Prose like this also stands for a dedication of spirit to the pursuit of knowledge and understanding. Ordinarily, though, the scientist's highly specialized technique puts his prose into a closed compartment; it may become a private language. Not necessarily: one remembers Faraday, and T. H. Huxley, from the last century. Sherrington's prose at its best is comparable with theirs.

THE eye-ball is a little camera. Its smallness is part of its perfection. A spheroid camera. There are not many anatomical organs where exact shape counts

for so much as with the eye. Light which will enter the
eye will traverse a lens placed in the right position
there. *Will* traverse; all this making of the eye which
will see in the light is carried out in the dark. It is a
preparing in darkness for use in light. The lens required is biconvex and is to be shaped truly enough to
focus its pencil of light at the particular distance of the
sheet of photosensitive cells at the back, the retina.
The biconvex lens is made of cells, like those of the
skin but modified to be glass-clear. It is delicately slung
with accurate centring across the path of the light
which *will* in due time some months later enter the eye.
In front of it a circular screen controls, like the iris-
stop of a camera or microscope, the width of the beam
and is adjustable, so that in a poor light more is taken
for the image. In microscope, or photographic camera,
this adjustment is made by the observer working the
instrument. In the eye this adjustment is automatic,
worked by the image itself!

The lens and screen cut the chamber of the eye into
a front half and a back half, both filled with clear
humour, practically water, kept under a certain pressure maintaining the eye-ball's right shape. The front
chamber is completed by a layer of skin specialized to
be glass-clear, and free from blood vessels which if
present would with their blood throw shadows within
the eye. This living glass-clear sheet is covered with a
layer of tear-water constantly renewed. This tear-water
has the special chemical power of killing germs which
might inflame the eye. This glass-clear bit of skin has
only one of the four-fold set of the skin-senses; its
touch is always "pain," for it should *not* be touched.

The skin above and below this window grows into movable flaps, dry outside like ordinary skin, but moist inside so as to wipe the window clean every minute or so from any specks of dust, by painting over it fresh tear-water.

We must not dwell on points of detail; our time precludes them, remarkable though they are. The light-sensitive screen at the back is the key-structure. It registers a continually changing picture. It receives, takes and records a moving picture life-long without change of "plate," through every waking day. It signals its shifting exposures to the brain.

This camera also focuses itself automatically, according to the distance of the picture interesting it. It makes its lens "stronger" or "weaker" as required. This camera also turns itself in the direction of the view required. It is moreover contrived as though with forethought of self-preservation. Should danger threaten, in a moment its skin shutters close protecting its transparent window. And the whole structure, with its prescience and all its efficiency, is produced by and out of specks of granular slime arranging themselves as of their own accord in sheets and layers, and acting seemingly on an agreed plan. That done, and their organ complete, they abide by what they have accomplished. They lapse into relative quietude and change no more. It all sounds an unskilful overstated tale which challenges belief. But to faithful observation so it is. There is more yet.

The little hollow bladder of the embryo-brain, narrowing itself at two points so as to be triple, thrusts from its foremost chamber to either side a hollow bud.

This bud pushes towards the overlying skin. That skin, as though it knew and sympathized, then dips down forming a cuplike hollow to meet the hollow brain stalk growing outward. They meet. The round end of the hollow brain-bud dimples inward and becomes a cup. Concurrently, the ingrowth from the skin nips itself free from its original skin. It rounds itself into a hollow ball, lying in the mouth of the brain-cup. Of this stalked cup, the optic cup, the stalk becomes in a few weeks a cable of a million nerve-fibres connecting the nerve-cells within the eye-ball itself with the brain. The optic cup, at first just a two-deep layer of somewhat simple-looking cells, multiplies its layers at the bottom of the cup where, when light enters the eye—which will not be for some weeks yet—the photo-image will in due course lie. There the layer becomes a four-fold layer of great complexity. It is strictly speaking a piece of the brain lying within the eye-ball. Indeed the whole brain itself, traced back to its embryonic beginning, is found to be all of a piece with the primordial skin—a primordial gesture as if to inculcate Aristotle's maxim about sense and mind.

The deepest cells at the bottom of the cup become a photo-sensitive layer—the sensitive film of the camera. If light is to act on the retina—and it is from the retina that light's visual effect is known to start—it must be absorbed there. In the retina a delicate purplish pigment absorbs incident light and is bleached by it, giving a light-picture. The photo-chemical effect generates nerve-currents running to the brain.

The nerve-lines connecting the photo-sensitive layer with the brain are not simple. They are in series of relays. It is the primitive cells of the optic cup, they and their progeny, which become in a few weeks these relays resembling a little brain, and each and all so shaped and connected as to transmit duly to the right points of the brain itself each light-picture momentarily formed and "taken." On the sense-cell layer the "image" has, picture-like, two dimensions. These space-relations "reappear" in the mind; hence we may think their data in the picture are in some way preserved in the electrical patterning of the resultant disturbance in the brain. But reminding us that the step from electrical disturbance in the brain to the mental experience is the mystery it is, the mind adds the third dimension when interpreting the two-dimensional picture! Also it adds colour; in short it makes a three-dimensional visual scene out of an electrical disturbance.

All this the cells lining the primitive optic cup have, so to say, to bear in mind, when laying these lines down. They lay them down by becoming them themselves.

Cajal, the gifted Spanish neurologist, gave special study to the retina and its nerve-lines to the brain. He turned to the insect-eye thinking the nerve-lines there "in relative simplicity" might display schematically, and therefore more readably, some general plan which Nature adopts when furnishing animal kind with sight. After studying it for two years this is what he wrote: "The complexity of the nerve-structures for vision is even in the insect something incredibly stupendous. From the insect's faceted eye proceeds an inextricable criss-cross of excessively slender nerve-fibres. These then plunge into a cell-labyrinth which doubtless serves to integrate what comes from the retinal layers. Next follow a countless host of amacrine cells and with them again numberless centrifugal fibres. All these elements are moreover so small the highest powers of the modern microscope hardly avail for following them. The intricacy of the connections defies description. Before it the mind halts, abased. *In tenuis labor*. Peering through the microscope into this Lilliputian life one wonders whether what we disdainfully term 'instinct' (Bergson's 'intuition') is not as Jules Fabre claims, life's crowning mental gift. Mind with instant and decisive action, the mind which in these tiny and ancient beings reached its blossom ages ago and earliest of all."

The first and greatest problem vision faces us with is doubtless that attaching to it as part of the matter-mind relation. How is it that the visual picture proceeds—if that is the right word—from an electrical disturbance in the brain? But as a sub-problem of high importance concerning vision comes that of pattern-vision. The study of vision, pursued comparatively in different animal forms, indicates that the primitive vision widely prevalent in simpler forms of life attains merely to the distinguishing of "light" from "no light." It usually reaches the refinement of distinguishing grades of intensity of light. This primitive vision however does not attain to distinguishing shape or figure. It does not arrive at what is called "pattern-vision." Our own seeing makes so rich a contribution to the shapes of our world that it is a little puzzling for us to think of unpatterned seeing. To think of colourless seeing is likewise a little difficult; in many creatures, however, sight is colourless.

Over a great diversity of more highly developed vision, the eye supplies a definite image of what it looks at. There we must suppose "pattern-vision"; without it the optical apparatus would seem wasted. In many cases the eye has means of focussing its image. That gives further development of the well-known relation between nerve and mind, namely that the "*place*" of a stimulated sensual point acts on the mind; whence "sensual space" with "local sign." It holds certainly not least in visual sense. If the sensitive sheet receiving the light-image be arranged as a mosaic of sub-areas corresponding severally with quasi-independent nerve-elements each with its access to "sense," then any light-image affecting two or more such sub-areas simultaneously begins to have "shape," or when affecting them successively begins to "move." The *spatial* pattern of the image thus acts on the mind. Different patterns acting differently enable mental distinction between them. For instance a moving object tends to "catch" vision.

We know enough of pattern-vision in ourselves to recognize that it is the foundation of a perceptual analysis of our visible world which is of supreme service to us. We know enough of our animal kith and kin to judge that in their case it serves not greatly otherwise for them. We must think that in each instance a great nervous rallying-place for confluent nerve-impulses from the quasi-independent elements of the ocular-sheet and for reactions between them must be appended to the eye. And that is what is found.

Serving the eye there are condensed masses of nerve-structure which examined by the microscope are thickets of seeming entanglement, doubtless replete with meaning could we read their scheme. These great nerve-ganglia of vision are familiar to the zoologist. He knows them in the ant, the bee, the squid, and most of all in our own stock, and especially in ourselves. Their complexity in the insect was what amazed even so veteran an anatomist as Cajal.

The human eye has about 137 million separate "seeing" elements spread out in the sheet of the retina. The number of nerve-lines leading from them to the brain gradually condenses down to little over a million. Each of these has in the brain, we must think, to find its right nerve-exchanges. Those nerve-exchanges lie far apart, and are but stations on the way to further stations. The whole crust of the brain is one thick tangled jungle of exchanges and of branching lines going thither and coming thence. As the eye's cup develops into the nervous retina all this intricate orientation to locality is provided for by corresponding growth in the brain. To compass what is needed adjacent cells, although sister and sister, have to shape themselves quite differently the one from the other. Most become patterned filaments, set lengthwise in the general direction of the current of travel. But some thrust out arms laterally as if to embrace together whole cables of the conducting system.

Nervous "conduction" is transmission of nervous signals, in this case to the brain. There is also another nervous process, which physiology was slower to discover. Activity at this or that point in the conducting system, where relays are introduced, can be decreased even to suppression. This lessening is called inhibition; it occurs in the retina as elsewhere. All this is arranged for by the developing eye-cap when preparing and carrying out its million-fold connections with the brain for the making of a seeing eye. Obviously there are almost illimitable opportunities for a false step. Such a false step need not count at the time because all that we have been considering is done months or weeks before the eye can be used. Time after time so perfectly is all performed that the infant eye is a good and fitting eye, and the mind soon is instructing itself and gathering knowledge through it. And the child's eye is not only an eye true to the human type, but an eye with personal likeness to its individual parent's. The millions of cells which made it have executed correctly a multitudinous dance engaging millions of performers in hundreds of sequences of particular different steps, differing for each performer according to his part. To picture the complexity and the precision beggars any imagery I have. But it may help us to think further.

There is too that other layer of those embryonic cells at the back of the eye. They act as the dead black lining of the camera; they with their black pigment kill any stray light which would blur the optical image. Further they shift their pigment. In full daylight they screen, and at night they unscreen, as wanted, the special see-ing elements which serve for seeing in dim light. These are the cells which manufacture the purple pigment, "visual purple," which sensitizes the eye for seeing in low light.

Then there is that little ball of cells which migrated from the skin and thrust itself into the mouth of the eye-stalk from the brain. It makes a lens there; it changes into glass-clear fibres, grouped with geometrical truth, locking together by toothed edges. To do the required pertains one would think to the optician's workshop rather than to a growing egg. The pencil of light let through must come to a point at the right distance for the length of the eye-ball which is to be. Not only must the lens be glass-clear but its shape must be optically right, and its substance must have the right optical refractive index. That index is higher than that of anything else which transmits light in the body. Well, it is attained. Its two curved surfaces back and front must be truly centred on one and the right axis, and each of the sub-spherical curvatures must be curved to the right degree, so that, the refractive index being right, light is brought to a focus on the retina and gives there a well-defined image. The optician obtains glass of the desired refractive index and skilfully grinds its curvatures in accordance with the mathematical formulae required. With the lens of the eye, a batch of granular skin-cells are told off to travel from the skin to which they strictly belong, to settle down in the mouth of the optic cup, to arrange themselves in a compact and geometrical ball, to turn into transparent fibres, to assume the right refractive index, and to make themselves into a sub-sphere with two correct curvatures truly centred on a certain axis. Thus it is they make a lens of the right size, set in the right place, that is, at the right distance behind the transparent window of the eye in front and the sensitive seeing screen of the retina behind. In short they behave as if fairly possessed.

I would not give a wrong impression. The optical apparatus of the eye is not all turned out with a precision equal to that of a first-rate optical workshop. It has defects which disarm the envy of the optician. It is rather as though the planet, producing all this as it does, worked under limitations. Regarded as a planet which "would," we yet find it no less a planet whose products lie open to criticism, in our case from themselves. Equally, on the other hand, in this very matter of the eye the process of its construction seems to seize opportunities offered by the peculiarity in some ways adverse, of the material it is condemned to use. It extracts from the untoward situation practical advantages for its instrument which human craftsmanship could never in that way provide. Thus the cells composing the core of this living lens are denser than those at the edge. This corrects a focussing defect inherent in ordinary glass-lenses. Again, the lens of the eye, compassing what no glass-lens can, changes its curvature to focus near objects as well as distant when wanted, for instance, when we read. An elastic capsule is spun over it and is arranged to be eased by aspecial muscle. Further, the pupil—the camera stop—is self-adjusting. All this without our having even to wish it; without even our knowing anything about it, beyond that we are seeing satisfactorily.

I must not weary you. As wonders, these things have grown stale through familiarity. The making of this eye out of self-actuated specks, which draw together and multiply and move as if obsessed with one desire, namely, to make the eye-ball. In a few weeks they have done so. Then, their madness over, they sit down and rest, satisfied to be life-long what they have made themselves, and, so to say, wait for death.

But the chief wonder of all we have not touched on yet. Wonder of wonders, though familiar even to boredom. So much with us that we forget it all our time. The eye sends, as we saw, into the cell-and-fibre forest of the brain throughout the waking day continual rhythmic streams of tiny, individually evanescent, electrical potentials. This throbbing streaming crowd of electrified shifting points in the spongework of the brain bears no obvious semblance in space-pattern, and even in temporal relation resembles but a little remotely the tiny two-dimensional upside-down picture of the outside world which the eye-ball paints on the beginnings of its nerve-fibres to the brain. But that little picture sets up an electrical storm. And that electrical storm so set up is one which affects a whole population of brain cells. Electrical charges having in themselves not the faintest elements of the visual—having, for instance, nothing of "distance," "right-side-upness," nor "vertical," nor "horizontal," nor "colour," nor "brightness," nor "shadow," nor "roundness," nor "squareness," nor "contour," nor "transparency," nor "opacity," nor "near," nor "far," nor visual anything—yet conjure up all these. A shower of little electrical leaks conjures up for me, when I look, the landscape; the castle on the height, or, when I look at him approaching, my friend's face, and how distant he is from me they tell me. Taking their word for it, I go forward and my other senses confirm that he is there.

A wonder of wonders which is a commonplace we take for granted. It is a case of "the world is too much with us"; too banal to wonder at. Those other things we paused over, the building and shaping of the eyeball, and the establishing of its nerve connections with the right points of the brain, all those other things and the rest pertaining to them we called in chemistry and physics to explain to us. And they did so, with promise of more help to come.

But this last, not the eye, but the "seeing" by the brain behind the eye? Physics and chemistry there are silent to our every question. All they say to us is that the brain is theirs, that without the brain which is theirs the seeing is not. But as to how? They vouchsafe us not a word.

From " Man on his Nature"

Such minute lucidity is exciting, and rare. Extreme clarity in the description of what the scientist sees and knows combines with a sense of wonder, of responsibility. This is a scientist in fine command of his material; yet he is a man whom the material itself astonishes, he has a feeling of awe before the evidence of his senses, and before the infinite complexity of those senses themselves. Those who find such prose exhilarating will find the description of the life cycle of the malaria parasite in the same book no less so. But it has to be confessed that there is not very much scientific prose of such distinction as this which the ordinary reader can hope to tackle profitably.

Atoms, Crystals and X-rays
William Bragg

The Gifford Lectures which provided the last reading have given us some of the best prose in modern philosophy and theology; they impose a duty to clarify deep thought into speech for a cultivated and various audience. The Christmas Lectures at the Royal Institution carry a similar obligation. It is "to explain as clearly as I can the discoveries of modern physical science" to a young and uninstructed audience. The words come from the introduction to Sir William Bragg's "Concerning the Nature of Things" from which the next two passages are taken. We find here, then, both the movement of the speaking voice (from which the best prose is never far removed) and that kind of simplicity of style that only the most thorough comprehension of what is to be explained makes possible. As with Sherrington, so here with Bragg: a sense of human purpose underlying the scientist's work gives the prose a particular distinction. He believed his audience would find the discoveries of modern physical science, once understood, "at the same time interesting and helpful: interesting because they display a beautiful order in the fundamental arrangement of Nature, and helpful because they have given us light on many old questions, and will surely help us with many that are new."

The modesty of the phrasing need not conceal the strength of the claim. Sir William Bragg was among the most important physicists of modern times. He was born in

Cumberland in 1862 and died in 1942. His son, Sir Lawrence Bragg, joined with him in his pioneering research into the structure of crystals and the movement of atoms, and in his discoveries about X-ray analysis of the structure of matter. Together they gained the Nobel Prize for Physics in 1915. Bragg became Director of the Royal Institution, and for many years arranged the Annual Christmas Lectures. So in his life, as in this prose, we can sense the connexion between laboratory and lecture hall; and detect something of the profound effect of scientific progress upon modern attitudes.

I

THE velocity with which the helium atom begins its flight is something like 10,000 miles in a second. In less than a minute it could get to the moon and back again if the speed were maintained, but the curious thing is that for all the speed and energy with which it starts it never gets far when it has to pass through anything material. Even if it is allowed to finish its course in the air, its speed has fallen to something of quite ordinary value after it has traversed a course of two or three inches in length. The course is, in general, perfectly straight, as we shall presently see in an actual experiment, and this is the very important point which we must consider with particular care. At first sight one does not realize how remarkable it is that its path should be *straight*: one thinks of a bullet fired through a block of wood, let us say, and making a cylindrical hole, or of the bullet in its straight course through the air. But the comparison is unfair. The bullet is a mass of lead enormously heavier than any molecule which it meets, and it brushes the air aside. But the helium atom is lighter and smaller than the atoms of nitrogen or oxygen of which the atmosphere is mainly composed, and we must think of some more truthful comparison. Suppose that a number of billiard balls are lying on a billiard table, and let them represent air molecules. If they are in movement the picture will be more correct, but the point does not really matter. Now let us drive a ball across the table aiming at a point on the opposite cushion, and watch what happens as the ball tries to get through the crowd that lies on the table, which crowd may or may not be in movement. It hits one of the balls and is turned to one side; it hits several in succession, and soon loses all trace of its original direction of movement. Shall we now drive it with all the force we can, and see whether it keeps any more nearly to the straight path? We try, and find that there is no improvement at all. The straight path cannot be obtained by any increase of speed, however great.

This picture or model is much more faithful than that of the moving bullet, and shows more clearly the remarkable nature of the radium effect. A helium atom must encounter a very large number of air molecules if it proceeds on a straight-line path, and if the atoms are of the size we have supposed them to be. In fact, the molecules lie far more thickly on the path than we can represent by the billiard-table model. It is possible to calculate how many air molecules, some oxygen, some nitrogen, would be pierced by a straight line three inches long drawn suddenly at any moment in the air, and the result is to be expressed in hundreds of thousands. How can the helium atom charge straight through this crowd, every member of which is heavier than itself? It does so, however, and we have to find some explanation.

Perhaps it might be thought that the straightness of the path is only apparent, and that if we could look into it in sufficient detail we should see that it was made up of innumerable zigzags made in going round the molecules met with. But a moment's reflection shows that the idea is absurd: the atom would need to possess the intelligence of a living being to give it the power of recovering a line once lost. If there were a cake shop on the opposite side of a crowded street, and if we gave a boy sixpence and directed him to the shop, he would no doubt pursue a path which was effectively straight, though it would be broken up by the need of dodging the various people and vehicles which the boy met with. But one cannot imagine an atom of helium doing anything of the sort.

There is only one way of explaining the marvel of the straight path: we must suppose that the helium atom goes *through* the molecules it meets, and that somehow it is enabled to do so by the fact that it is moving at such an unusual speed. It is a very startling idea. However, no other suggests itself; and, as a matter of fact, it turns out that we can explain many other things by its aid. Consequently, we feel sure that we are on the right track.

It is time now that we should see this effect with our own eyes: the conclusion at which we have arrived is so new and so full of meaning that we would like to have an experimental demonstration if possible, and convince ourselves of the reality of these straight-line paths. We owe to Mr C. T. R. Wilson a beautiful piece of apparatus which gives us a vivid picture of what happens, and we will make use of it at once. The experiment is, in my opinion, one of the most wonderful in the world of science. We are going to see the actual tracks of separate helium atoms, each of which begins its course at a speed of ten thousand miles a second and yet completes it after traversing about three inches of air. But we must first enter upon some explanation of how the apparatus works; for there are ingenious devices in it.

There is a cylindrical box of brass, with a glass top and a base which can be raised or lowered so as to alter the depth of the box. There is a machinery of wheels, cranks and levers by which the bottom of the box can be suddenly dropped at convenient intervals. Whenever this happens, the air or other gas which the box contains is chilled by the sudden expansion. We shall study effects of this kind more carefully in the next lecture. At the side of the box, in its interior, a minute speck of radium is mounted on a suitable holder. Every moment some of its atoms break up and expel atoms of helium, of which a certain number are shot straight into the box. The diameter of the box is big enough to allow the atoms to finish their courses in the air within. The average life of radium is so long that even if the apparatus held together for two thousand years, half of the radium speck would still be left. Yet each second, ten, twenty or a hundred atoms disappear in the expulsion of the helium atoms. Perhaps in no better way can it be shown how many atoms are concentrated in a small compass.

The air in the chamber is kept damp, consequently the chill due to expansion tends to produce a fog. Fog when it has to settle prefers to deposit itself on a solid nucleus of some sort, rather than to form independent drops in the air. The small particles of dust, if there are any, are made use of, which is the reason why fogs so readily form in a dirty atmosphere. But of all things moisture prefers to settle on those atoms through which the helium atom has passed. The reason is that the atom is temporarily damaged by the transit: a small portion has generally been chipped away. The portion removed is what we now call an "electron"; it is charged with negative electricity, and the atom which has lost it is correspondingly charged with positive electricity. The electron set free settles on some neighbouring atom, sooner or later; and in consequence there are two charged atoms, one positive and one negative, where previously there were no charged atoms at all. The charged atoms have a great attraction for moisture, and the fog forms on them in preference to anything else. If, therefore, a helium atom has just made its straight road through the gas, and has left behind it numbers of charged atoms on its track, and if, at that moment, the sudden expansion causes a chill, fog settles along the track. A bright light is made to illuminate the chamber, so that the fog tracks are visible as bright straight lines, showing against the blackened background of the bottom of the cylindrical chamber. They last a few seconds, and then the fog particles slowly disperse. If the helium atom completes its track just before the fog is formed, the line is sharp and clear; because the charged atoms have not had time to wander from the track. But if the track is made some time before the expansion, the line of fog is more diffuse. It is to be remembered that the helium atoms are being shot out all the time, day and night; but it is only when an expansion is made that tracks are made visible.

If we watch the successive expansions, we see that the tracks, though quite straight over large parts of their course, do undergo at times sudden sharp deflection, especially when they are nearing the end. This remarkable effect turns out to be most important, and we must refer to it presently.

Let us now try to picture to ourselves in what way we must modify our first conception of the atom so that we can explain the effects we now see. The atoms must be so constituted that when they meet one another in the ordinary way, as, for example, when molecules of oxygen collide in the atmosphere, they behave as if each had a domain of its own into which no other might enter. Or, when they are pressed together, as in a solid, they occupy as a whole an amount of space which is sufficient to make room for them all. But when one atom—the helium atom is our chief example—is hurled against others with sufficient speed, the one atom goes through the other, as if the defences round the domains had been broken down. We find a satisfactory explanation when we imagine each atom to be like a solar system in miniature. There is to be a nucleus, corresponding to the sun, and round the nucleus there are to be satellites or planets, which we call electrons. The nucleus is charged with positive electricity; each electron is charged with negative electricity, and all electrons are alike. The positive charge on the nucleus is just enough to balance the united negative charges of the electrons. The electrons are supposed to be in movement, just as the planets are revolving round the sun, but the movements are no doubt complicated, and their nature need not for the moment concern us at all.

Instead, therefore, of a round hard ball of a certain size, which was our first rough picture of an atom, we have something like a solar system in miniature. We can at once see how one atom of this kind can pass through another, just as we might imagine one solar system passing through another, without injury to either provided that no one body of one system made a direct hit on a body of the other and that the motion was quick enough. The latter condition is necessary because if one solar system stayed too long inside or in the neighbourhood of another there would certainly be very serious disturbances of the courses of the planets.

But then, we may ask, how can an atom, if this be its nature, have the power of keeping another outside its own domain? How can it appropriate any portion of space to itself, and prevent the intrusion of another atom when the speed at which they meet is low? The explanation becomes clear when we consider the special arrangement of the positive and negative charges. Every atom is surrounded by a shell or cloak of electrons; and, when two atoms collide, it is their shells which first come close together. Since like charges of electricity repel one another, the two atoms will experience a force which tends to keep them apart:

in other words, they will resist encroachment on their own domains. This is, no doubt, a very rough picture of what actually happens, and as a matter of fact it is difficult to explain the strength of the resisting forces on such a simple hypothesis. Still, it is on the right lines, no doubt. When the two atoms approach each other at a high speed, the system of electrons and nucleus of one atom slip through those of the other.

II

We may now ask ourselves why, if the natural arrangement of molecules is regular, we do not find all bodies in crystalline form. To this we must answer that in the first place a large perfect crystal must grow from a single nucleus. It is difficult to say what first arrests the relative motion of two or three molecules of the cooling liquid, joining them together and making a beginning to which other molecules become attached. Perhaps it is a mere accident of their meeting; perhaps some minute particle of foreign matter is present which serves as a base, or some irregularity on the wall of the containing vessel. If there are very many nuclei present in the liquid, very many crystals will grow; and since they are not likely to be orientated to each other when they meet, they will finally form an indefinite mass of small crystals, not a single crystal. They may be so small that to the eye the whole appears as a solid mass without any regularity of form. In order that a large perfect crystal should be formed, the arrangements must be such that the molecules find few centres on which to grow. And they must grow, usually, very slowly and quietly, so that each molecule has time to settle itself correctly in its proper place. The molecules must have enough movement to permit of this adjustment. These conditions are well shown in the methods which the crystallographer employs for the growth of crystals. If, for example, he is growing a large crystal of salt from a solution of brine, he will suspend a minute, well-formed crystal in the brine, and he will keep the temperature of the latter so carefully adjusted that the atoms of sodium and chlorine are only tempted to give up their freedom when they meet an assemblage of atoms already in perfect array—that is to say, when they come across the suspended crystal. If the solution is too hot, the suspended crystal will be dissolved in the unsaturated solution; if it is too cold, crystals will begin to grow at many points. Sometimes the liquid is kept in gentle movement so that various parts of it are brought to the suspended crystal in due turn. The principal conditions are time and quiet, a solution of the salt just ready to precipitate its contents, temperature and strength of solution being properly adjusted for the purpose, the presence of a small perfect crystal and the gentle movement of the solution past it. We do not, of course, quite understand how these or some such conditions come to be realized during the growth of a diamond or a ruby; but we find them to be necessary in the laboratory when we attempt to grow crystals ourselves.

When the conditions are fulfilled in part only, we may get a mass of minute crystals in disarray; we may even find a totally irregular structure—an amorphous substance, to employ the usual phrase. This alone would account for the seeming rarity of crystals, and we have also to bear in mind that many bodies are highly composite in character, consisting of many substances each of which has its own natural form. The X-rays show us that the crystal is not so rare as we have been inclined to think; that even in cases where there is no obvious crystallization Nature has been attempting to produce regular arrangements, and that we have missed them hitherto because our means of detecting them have been inefficient. The regularity of Nature's arrangement is manifested in the visible crystal, but is also to be discovered elsewhere. It is this regularity which we shall see to be one of the foundation elements of the success of the new methods of analysis.

Let us now turn to the consideration of the X-rays. The reason of their ability to help us at this stage may first be given in general terms.

The X-rays are a form of light, from which they differ in wave length only. The light waves which are sent out by the sun or an electric light or a candle and are perceived by our eyes have a narrow range of magnitude. The length of the longest is about a thirty-thousandth of an inch, and of the shortest about half as much. These sizes are well suited to the purpose for which we employ them. Let us remember that when we see an object we do so by observing the alterations which the object makes in the light coming from the source and reaching our eyes by way of the object. Our eyes and brains have attained by long practice a marvellous skill in detecting and interpreting such changes. We may be unsuccessful, however, if the object is too small; and this is not only because a small object necessarily makes a small change in the light. There is a second and more subtle reason: the *nature* of the effect is changed when the dimensions of the object are about the same as the length of the wave, or are still less. Let us imagine ourselves to be walking on the seashore watching the incoming waves. We come in the course of our walk to a place where the strength of the waves is less, and when we look for the reason we observe a reef out to sea which is sheltering the beach. We have a parallel to an optical shadow: the distant storm which has raised the waves may be compared to the sun, the shore on which the waves beat is like the illuminated earth, and the reef is like a cloud which casts a shadow. The optical shadow enables us to detect the presence of the cloud, and the silence on the shore makes us suspect the presence of the reef. Now the dimensions of the reef are probably much greater than the length of the wave. If for the reef were substituted a pole planted in the bottom of the sea and standing out of the surface, the effect would be too small to observe. This is, of course, obvious. Even, however, if a very large number of poles were so planted in the sea so that the effect mounted up and was as great as that of the reef, the resulting shadow would tell us nothing about each individual pole. The diameter of the pole is too small compared with the length of the wave to impress any permanent characteristic on it; the wave sweeps by and closes up again and there is an end of it. If, however, the sea were smooth except for a tiny ripple caused by a breath of wind, each pole could cast a shadow which would persist for at least a short distance to the lee of the pole.

The width of the ripple is less than the diameter of the pole, and there is therefore a shadow to each pole.

Just so light waves sweeping over molecules much smaller than themselves receive no impressions which can be carried to the eye and brain so as to be perceived as the separate effects of the molecules. And it is no use trying to overcome our difficulty by any instrumental aids. The microscope increases our power of perceiving small things: with its help we may, perhaps, detect objects thousands of times smaller than we could perceive with the naked eye. But it fails when we try to see things which are of the same size as the wave length of light, and no increase in skill of manufacture will carry us further. But the X-rays are some ten thousand times finer than ordinary light, and, provided suitable and sensitive substitutes can be found for the eyes, may enable us to go ten thousand times deeper into the minuteness of structure. This brings us comfortably to the region of atoms and molecules, which have dimensions in the various directions of the order of a hundred-millionth of an inch, and this is also the order of the wave lengths of X-rays. Broadly speaking, the discovery of X-rays has increased the keenness of our vision ten thousand times, and, we can now "see" the individual atoms and molecules.

We must now connect the X-rays with the crystal, and again we may first state the point in a broad way. Although the single molecule can now affect the X-rays just as in our analogy the single pole can cast a shadow of the fine ripples, yet the single effect is too minute. In the crystal, however, there is an enormous number of molecules in regular array, and it may happen that when a train of X-rays falls upon the crystal the effects on the various molecules are combined and so become sensible. Again, we may make use of analogy. If a single soldier made some movement with his rifle and bayonet, it might happen that a flash in the sunlight, caused by the motion, was unobserved a mile away on account of its small magnitude. But if the soldier was one of a body of men marching in the same direction in close order, who all did the same thing at the same time, the combined effect might be easily seen. The fineness of X-rays makes it possible for each atom or molecule to have some effect, and the regular arrangement of the crystal adds all the effects together.

From "Concerning the Nature of Things"

The prose is as careful, as assiduous, as measured, as the scientist himself had to be, pursuing his own research into the structure of crystals. But again you feel the deep respect behind the descriptions, respect for 'the beautiful order in the fundamental arrangement of Nature.' It reminds us that Bragg was himself among the discoverers whose findings he describes. In its way, "Concerning the Nature of Things" is unique, as "Man on his Nature" is unique. But the Christmas Lectures have included such prose classics as Faraday's "Chemical History of a Candle." Bragg himself gave two other series, "The World of Sound" (Bell) and "Old Trades and new Knowledge." This last is of particular interest for its connexion with "The Wheelwright's Shop." "And I must admit," he says in introduction, "that my lectures are meant to have a moral, in that there is much more than fascination in the history of men's work; there is also the plain and urgent lesson that we must continually improve our old handicrafts by means of the new knowledge which is always flowing in. Also, there is an ideal which may seem far beyond us, and yet must always be aimed at: it is this, to give everybody work to do, and make everybody enjoy doing it well." Bragg shares a common wisdom with Sturt and Gill. The scientific attitude as he represents it, and his prose speaks for it, is based in a deep sense of human responsibility.

VI

The Human Spirit
and the Natural World

Edward Thomas : *The South Country*

D. H. Lawrence : *Phoenix*

The Spirit of Place
Edward Thomas

These two descriptive passages come from Edward Thomas's book, "The South Country," composed in 1909. Of the several poets whose work in prose appears among these readings, Edward Thomas is considerably the finest. He was born of Welsh parents in 1878. He married while an undergraduate at Oxford, and made writing his profession. Books and articles, especially about the countryside and country life (which he came to know intimately, walking much) came fast from him; but they provided a precarious livelihood. Only in 1914, urged to it by the American poet Robert Frost, did he begin seriously to write poetry. Then came the war: he enlisted in 1915; in April 1917 he was killed at Arras.

His poetry takes its origin, most often, in solitude, quiet, and natural life: but beneath that surface it is a self-searching poetry of peculiar honesty. The quiet tone conceals reserves of strength and independence; the original rhythms and conversational idiom reveal unusual sensuous alertness. And deep, fresh, sincere sensuous response gives life and savour to his prose as well. It has not the final naturalness of his best poetry; yet its eagerness and visible detail give it worth on its own account.

Here, then, is the human spirit responding in another way—with all the vitality of the senses, and the attendant quickening of memory and reflection—to the world about it.

I

In Cornwall, where the wrinkles and angles of the earth's age are left to show, antiquity plays a giant's part on every hand. What a curious effect have those ruins, all but invisible among the sands, the sea-blue scabious, the tamarisk and rush, though at night they seem not inaudible when the wild air is full of crying! Some that are not nearly as old are almost as magical. One there is that stands near a great water, cut off from a little town and from the world by a round green hill and touched by no road but only by a wandering path. At the foot of this hill, among yellow mounds of sand, under blue sky, the church is dark and alone. It is not very old—not five centuries—and is of plainest masonry: its blunt short spire of slate slabs that leans slightly to one side, with the smallest of perforated slate windows at the base, has a look of age and rusticity. In the churchyard is a rough grey cross of stone—a disc supported by a pillar. It is surrounded by the waving noiseless tamarisk. It looks northward over the sandhills at a blue bay, guarded on the west by tall grey cliffs which a white column surmounts.

For a time the nearer sandhills have rested and clothed themselves in bird's-foot trefoil, thyme, eyebright and short turf: but once the church was buried beneath them. Between the round hill and the church a tiny stream sidles along through a level hiding-place of flags and yellow flag flowers, of purple figwort and purply orchis and green grass.

A cormorant flies low across the sky—that sable bird which seems to belong to the old time, the time of badger and beaver, of ancient men who rose up out of the crags of this coast. To them, when the cuckoo first called one April, came over the blue sea a small brown ship, followed by three seals, and out of it descended a Christian from Ireland, black-haired, blue-eyed, with ready red lips and deep sweet voice and spoke to them, all alone. He told them of a power that ruled the blue waters and shifting sands, who could move the round green hill to the rock of the white gulls; taller and grimmer than the cloven headland yet sweet and gentle as the fennel above; deep-voiced as the Atlantic storm, tender also as the sedge-warbler in the flags below the hill; whose palace was loftier than the blue to which the lark was now soaring, milder and richer than the meadows in May and everlasting; and his attendants were more numerous and bright than the herring under a moon of frost. The milk-pails should be fuller and the grass deeper and the corn heavier in the ear if they believed in this; the pilchards should be as water boiling in the bay; and they should have wings as of the white birds that lounged about the precipices of the coast. And all the time the three seals lay with their heads and backs above the shallows and watched. Perhaps the men believed his word; perhaps they dropped him over the precipice to see whether he also flew like a gull: but here is the church named after him.

All along the coast (and especially where it is lofty and houseless, and on the ledges of the crags the young grey gulls unable to fly bob their heads seaward and

try to scream like their parents who wheel far and near
with double yodeling cry), there are many rounded
barrows looking out to sea. And there are some amidst
the sand-hills, bare and corrugated by the wind and
heaved up like a feather-bed, their edges golden against
the blue sky or mangily covered by drab marram grass
that whistles wintrily; and near by the blue sea,
slightly roughened as by a harrow, sleeps calm but
foamy among cinder-coloured isles; donkeys graze on
the brown turf, larks rise and fall and curlews go by;
a cuckoo sings among the deserted mines. But the
barrows are most noble on the high heather and grass.
The lonely turf is full of lilac scabious flowers and
crimson knapweed among the solid mounds of gorse.
The brown-green-grey of the dry summer grass reveals
myriads of the flowers of thyme, of stonecrop yellow
and white, of pearly eyebright, of golden lady's fingers,
and the white or grey clover with its purest and
earthiest of all fragrances. Here and there steep tracks
descend slantwise among the thrift-grown crags to the
sea, or promise to descend but end abruptly in precipices. On the barrows themselves, which are either
isolated or in a group of two or three, grow thistle and
gorse. They command mile upon mile of cliff and sea.
In their sight the great headlands run out to sea and
sinking seem to rise again a few miles out in a sheer
island, so that they resemble couchant beasts with
backs under water but heads and haunches upreared.
The cliffs are cleft many times by steep-sided coves,
some with broad sand and shallow water among purple
rocks, the outlet of a rivulet, others ending precipi-
tously so that the stream suddenly plunges into the

black sea among a huddle of sunless boulders. Near such a stream there will be a grey farm amid grey out-buildings—with a carved wooden eagle from the wreckage of the cove, or a mermaid, once a figure-head with fair long hair and round bosom, built into the wall of a barn. Or there is a briny hamlet grouped steeply on either side of the stream which gurgles among the pebbles down to the feet of the bearded fisherman and the ships a-gleam. Or perhaps there is no stream at all, and bramble and gorse come down dry and hot to the lips of the emerald and purple pools. Deep roads from the sea to the cliff-top have been worn by smuggler and fisherman and miner, climbing and descending. Inland shows a solitary pinnacled church tower, rosy in the warm evening—a thin line of trees, long bare stems and dark foliage matted—and farther still the ridges of misty granite, rough as the back of a perch.

Of all the rocky land, of the sapphire sea white with quiet foam, the barrows are masters. The breaking away of the rock has brought them nearer to the sea as it has annihilated some and cut off the cliff-ways in mid-career. They stand in the unenclosed waste and are removed from all human uses and from most way-faring. Thus they share the sublimity of beacons and are about to show that tombs also have their deaths. Linnet and stonechat and pipit seem to attend upon them, with pretty voices and motions and a certain ghastliness, as of shadows, given to their cheerful and sudden flittings by the solemn neighbourhood. But most of their hold upon the spirit they owe to their powerful suggestion that here upon the high sea border was once lived a bold proud life, like that of Beowulf, whose words, when he was dying from the wounds of his last victory, were: "Bid the warriors raise a funeral mound to flash with fire on a promontory above the sea, that it may stand high and be a memorial by which my people shall remember me, and seafarers driving their tall ships through the mist of the sea shall say: 'Beowulf's Mound.'"

In Cornwall as in Wales, these monuments are the more impressive, because the earth, wasting with them and showing her bones, takes their part. There are days when the age of the Downs, strewn with tumuli and the remnants of camp and village, is incredible; or rather they seem in the course of long time to have grown smooth and soft and kind, and to be, like a rounded languid cloud, an expression of Earth's summer bliss of afternoon. But granite and slate and sandstone jut out, and in whatsoever weather speak rather of the cold, drear, hard, windy dawn. Nothing can soften the lines of Trendreen or Brown Willy or Carn Galver against the sky. The small stone-hedged ploughlands amidst brake and gorse do but accentuate the wildness of the land from which they have been won. The deserted mines are frozen cries of despair as if they had perished in conflict with the waste; and in a few years their chimneys standing amidst rotted woodwork, the falling masonry, the engine rusty, huge and still (the abode of rabbits, and all overgrown with bedstraw, the stern thistle and wizard henbane) are in keeping with the miles of barren land, littered with rough silvered stones among heather and furze, whose many barrows are deep in fern and bramble and foxglove. The cotton grass raises its pure nodding white. The old roads dive among still more furze and bracken and bramble and foxglove, and on every side the land grows no such crop as that of grey stones. Even in the midst of occasional cornfield or weedless pasture a long grey upright stone speaks of the past. In many places men have set up these stones, roughly squaring some of them, in the form of a circle or in groups of circles —and over them beats the buzzard in slow hesitating and swerving flight. In one place the work of Nature might be mistaken for that of man. On a natural hillock stands what appears to be the ruin of an irregularly heaped wall of grey rock, roughened by dark-grey lichen, built of enormous angular fragments like the masonry of a giant's child. Near at hand, bracken, pink stonecrop, heather and bright gold tormentil soften it; but at a distance it stands black against the summer sky, touched with the pathos of man's handiwork overthrown, yet certainly an accident of Nature. It commands Cape Cornwall and the harsh sea, and St Just with its horned church tower. On every hand lie cromlech, camp, circle, hut and tumulus of the unwritten years. They are confused and mingled with the natural litter of a barren land. It is a silent Bedlam of history, a senseless cemetery or museum, amidst which we walk as animals must do when they see those valleys full of skeletons where their kind are said to go punctually to die. There are enough of the dead; they outnumber the living; and there those trite truths burst with life and drum upon the tympanum with ambiguous fatal voices. At the end of this many-barrowed moor, yet not in it, there is a solitary circle of grey stones, where the cry of the past is less vociferous, less bewildering, than on the moor itself, but more intense. Nineteen tall, grey stones stand round a taller, pointed one that is heavily bowed, amidst long grass and bracken and furze. A track passes close by, but does not enter the circle; the grass is unbent except by the weight of its bloom. It bears a name that connects it with the assembling and rivalry of the bards of Britain. Here, under the sky, they met, leaning upon the stones, tall, fair men of peace, but half-warriors, whose songs could change ploughshare into sword. Here they met, and the growth of the grass, the perfection of the stones (except that one stoops as with age), and the silence, suggest that since the last bard left it, in robe of blue or white or green—the colours of sky and cloud and grass upon this fair day—the circle has been unmolested, and the law obeyed which forbade any but a bard to enter it. Sky-blue was the colour of a chief bard's robe, emblematic of peace and heavenly calm, and of unchangeableness. White, the colour of the Druid's dress, was the emblem of light, and of its correlatives, purity of conduct, wisdom, and piety. Green was the colour of the youthful ovate's robe, for it was the emblem of growth. Their uniformity of colour signified perfect truth. And the inscription upon the chair of the bards of Beisgawen was, "Nothing is that is not for ever and ever." Blue and white and green, peace and light and growth—"Nothing is that is not for ever and ever"—these things and the blue sky, the white, cloudy hall of the sun, and the green bough and grass, hallowed the ancient stones, and clearer than any vision of tall bards in the morning of the world was the tranquil delight of being thus "teased out of time" in the presence of this ancientness.

It is strange to pass from these monumental moors straight to the sea which records the moments, not the years or the centuries. In fine weather especially its colour—when, for example, it is faintly corrugated and of a blue that melts towards the horizon into such a hue that it is indistinguishable from the violet wall of dawn—is a perpetual astonishment on account of its unearthliness and evanescence. The mind does not at once accept the fact that here underneath our eyes is, as it were, another sky. The physical act of looking up induces a special mood of solemnity and veneration, and during the act the eyes meet with a fitting object in the stainless heavens. Looking down we are used to seeing the earth, the road, the footpath, the floor, the hearth; but when, instead, it is the sea and not any of these things, although our feet are on firm land, the solemnity is of another kind. In its anger the sea becomes humanized or animalized: we see resemblances to familiar things. There is, for instance, an hour sometimes after sunset, when the grey sky coldly lights the lines of white plumes on a steely sea, and they have an inevitable likeness to a trampling chivalry that charges upon a foe. But a calm sea is incomparable except to moods of the mind. It is then as remote from the earth and earthly things as the sky, and the remoteness is the more astonishing because it is almost within our grasp. It is no wonder that a great idea was expressed by the fortunate islands in the sea. The youthfulness, the incorruptibility of the sea, continually

renewing itself, the same from generation to generation, prepares it as a fit sanctuary of the immortal dead.
So at least we are apt to think at certain times, coming
from the heavy, scarred, tormented earth to that
immense aèry plain of peacock blue. And yet at other
times that same unearthliness will suggest quite other
thoughts. It has not changed and shrunken and grown
like the earth; it is not sun-warmed: it is a monster that
has lain unmoved by time, sleeping and moaning outside the gates within which men and animals have
become what they are. Actually that cold fatal element
and its myriad population without a sound brings a
wistfulness into the mind as if it could feel back and
dimly recall the dawn of time when the sea was incom-
prehensible and impassable, when the earth had but
lately risen out of the waters and was yet again to
descend beneath: it becomes a type of the waste where
everything is unknown or uncertain except death,
pouring into the brain the thoughts that men have had
on looking out over untrodden mountain, forest,
swamp, in the drizzling dawn of the world. The sea is
exactly what it was when mountain, forest, swamp
were imperturbable enemies, and the sight of it restores
the ancient fear. I remember one dawn above all others
when this restoration was complete. When it was yet
dark the wind rose gustily under a low grey sky and a
lark sang amidst the moan of gorse and the creak of
gates and the deeply taken breath of the tide at the full.
Nor was it yet light when the gulls began to wheel and
wind and float with a motion like foam on a whirlpool
or inter-woven snow. They wheeled about the masts
of fishing-boats that nodded and kissed and crossed in

a steep cove of crags whose black edges were slavered
by the foam of the dark sea; and there were no men
among the boats or about the grey houses that looked
past the walls of the cove to the grim staircase and sea-
doors of a black headland, whose perpendicular rocks
stood up far out of the reach of the wings fashioned in
the likeness of gigantic idols. The higher crags were
bushy and scaly with lichen, and they were cushioned
upon thrift and bird's-foot trefoil and white bladder
campion. It was a bristling sea, not in the least stormy,
but bristling dark and cold through the slow colourless dawn, dark and cold and immense; and at the edge
of it the earth knelt, offering up the music of a small
flitting bird and the beauty of small flowers, white and
gold, to those idols. They were terrible enough. But
the sea was more terrible; for it was the god of whom
those rocks were the poor childish images, and it
seemed that the god had just then disclosed his true
nature and hence the pitiful loveliness of the flowers,
the pitiful sweetness of the bird that sang among the
rocks at the margin of the kind earth.

II

First beeches line the rising and descending road—
past a church whose ivied tombstones commemorate
men of Cornish name—as far as an inn and a sycamore
nobly balanced upon a pedestal of matted roots. Then
there are ash-trees on either side and ricks of straw
wetted to an orange hue, and beyond them the open
cornland, and rising out of it an all-day-long procession
in the south the great company of the Downs again,

some tipped with wood, some bare; in the north, a broken chain of woods upon low but undulating land seem the vertebrae of a forest of old time stretching from east to west like the Downs. Hither and thither the drunken pewits cry over the furrows, and thousands of rooks and daws wheel over the stubble. As the day grows old it grows sweet and golden and the rain ceases, and the beauty of the Downs in the humid clearness does not long allow the eyes to wander away from them. At first, when the sun breaks through, all silver bright and acclaimed by miles of clouds in his own livery, the Downs below are violet, and have no form except where they carve the sky with their long arches. It is the woods northward that are chiefly glorified by the light and warmth, and the glades penetrating them and the shining stubble and the hedges, and the flying wood-pigeons and the cows of richest brown and milky white; the road also gleams blue and wet. But as the sun descends the light falls on the Downs out of a bright cave in the gloomy forest of sky, and their flanks are olive and their outlines intensely clear. From one summit to another runs a string of trees like cavalry connecting one beech clump with another, so that they seem actually to be moving and adding themselves to the clumps. Above all is the abstract beauty of pure line—coupled with the beauty of the serene and the uninhabited and remote—that holds the eye until at length the hills are humbled and dispread as part of the ceremony of sunset in a tranquil, ensanguined, quietly travelling sky. The blue swallows go slowly along the silent road beside me, and the last rays bless a grooved common grazed upon

by cows and surrounded by ranges of low white buildings and a row of lichened grotesque limes, dark of
bole, golden-leaved, where children are playing and an
anvil rings.

Frost follows after the blue silence and chill of twilight, and the dawn is dimmest violet in a haze that
reveals the candid grass, the soaking blue dark elms
painted yellow only in one place, the red roofs, all in
a world of the unborn, and the waters steaming around
invisible crying coots. Gradually round white clouds
—so dim that the sky seems but to dream of round
white clouds—appear imbedded in the haze; the beams
grow hot, and a breeze joins with them in sucking and
scattering all the sweet of the first fallen leaves, the
weed fires and the late honeysuckle.

Why are there no swifts to race and scream? We fret
over these stages of the descending year; we dream on
such a day as this that there is no need of farther
descent. We would preserve those days of the reaping;
we have lost them; but we recall them now when the
steam-plough has furrowed the sheeny stubble, and
long for the day when the gentle north wind can only
just stir the clusters of aspen-leaves, and the branches
are motionless. The nut bushes hang dreamily, heavily,
over the white cool roads. The wood-pigeon's is the
sole voice in the oak woods of the low hills, except that
once or twice a swift screams as he pursues that martial
flight of his—as of one who swings a sword as he goes
—towards the beeches and hop gardens of the higher
hills in the north; it is perhaps the last day for more
than eight months that his cry will be heard. A few
barley-straws hang from the hazels; some leaves are

yellow. Autumn, in fact, seems possible to the mind that is not perfectly content with these calm sweet airs and the sense of the fulness of things.

At a crossing a small island is made amidst this and three other roads, and on the island stands an oast house with two mellow cones and white leaning cowls; and beside it a simple tiled cart-lodge, dimly displaying massive wheels, curving bulwarks of waggons and straight shafts behind its doorless pillars of rough-hewn wood. Making one group with these, though separated from them by one road, is an old red farm-house, of barely distinguishable timber and brick, with white-edged dormers and lower windows and doors, entrenched behind hollyhocks of deepest red and the burning discs of everlasting sunflowers. Behind the gates stand four haystacks brightly thatched, and one that is dark and old and carved into huge stairs.

Notice the gate into the rickyard. It is of the usual five oak bars; and across these is a diagonal bar from the lowest and nearest the hinge to the upper end of the opposite side, and from top to bottom a perpendicular cross-bar divides the gate. The top bar marks it as no common gate made at a factory with a hundred others of the same kind, though there are scores of them in Kent. It thickens gradually towards the hinge end of the gate, and then much more decidedly so that it resembles a gun barrel and stock; and just where the stock begins it is carved with something like a trigger-guard; the whole being well proportioned, graceful but strong. In all the best gates of Kent, Sussex and Surrey and the South Country there is an approach to this form, usually without the trigger-guard, but sometimes having instead a much more elaborate variation of it which takes away from the dignity and simplicity of the gate. At the road's edge crooked quince-trees lean over a green pond and green but nearly yellow straight reeds; and four cart-horses, three sorrels and a grey, are grouped under one stately walnut.

These things mingle their power with that of the silence and the wooded distance under the blue and rosy west. The slow dying of a train's roar beats upon the shores of the silence and the distance, and is swallowed up in them like foam in sand, and adds one more trophy to the glory of the twilight.

Night passes, and the white dawn is poured out over the dew from the folds in low clouds of infinitely modulated grey. Autumn is clearly hiding somewhere in the long warm alleys under the green and gold of the hops. The very colours of the oast houses seem to wait for certain harmonies with oaks in the meadows and beeches in the steep woods. The songs, too, are those of the drowsy yellow-hammer, of the robin moodily brooding in orchards yellow spotted and streaked, of the unseen wandering willow-wren singing sweetly but in a broken voice of a matter now forgotten, of the melancholy twit of the single bullfinch as he flies. The sudden lyric of the wren can stir no corresponding energy in the land which is bowed, still, comfortable, like a deep-uddered cow fastened to the milking-stall and munching grains. Soon will the milk and honey flow. The reaping machine whirrs; the wheelwrights have mended the waggons' wheels and patched their sides; they stand outside their lodges.

There is a quarter of a sloping wheat-field reaped;

the shocks stand out above the silvery stubble in the evening like rocks out of a moonlight sea. The un-reaped corn is like a tawny coast; and all is calm, with the quiet of evening heavens fallen over the earth. This beauty of the ripe Demeter standing in the August land is incomparable. It reminds one of the poet who said that he had seen a maid who looked like a fountain on a green lawn when the south wind blows in June; and one whose smile was as memorable as the new moon in the first still mild evening of the year, when it is seen for a moment only over the dark hills; and one whose walking was more kindling to the blood than good ale by a winter fire on an endless evening among friends; but that now he has met another, and when he is with her or thinks of her he becomes as one that is blind and deaf to all other things.

But a few days and the bryony leaves are palest yellow in the hedge. Rooks are innumerable about the land, but their cawing, like all other sounds, like all the early bronze and rose and gold of the leaves, is muffled by the mist which endures right through the afternoon; and all day falls the gentle rain. In the hillside hop garden two long lines of women and children, red and white and black, are destroying the golden green of the hops, and they are like two caterpillars destroying a leaf. Pleasant it is now to see the white smoke from the oast house pouring solidly like curving plumes into the still rain, and to smell the smell, bitter and never to be too much sniffed and enjoyed, that travels wide over the fields. For the hop drier has lit his two fires of Welsh coal and brimstone and charcoal under the two cones of the oast house, and has spread his couch of straw on the floor where he can sleep his many little sleeps in the busy day and night. The oast house consists of the pair of cones, white-vaned and tiled, upon their two circular chambers in which the fires are lit. Attached to these on one side is a brick building of two large rooms, one upon the ground, where the hop drier sleeps and tends his fires, lighted only by doors at either side and divided by the wooden pillars which support the floor of the upper room. This, the oast chamber, reached by a ladder, is a beautiful room, its oak boards polished by careful use and now stained faintly by the green-gold of hops, its roof raftered and high and dim. Light falls upon it on one side from two low windows, on the opposite side from a door through which the hops arrive from the garden. The waggon waits below the door, full of the loose, stained hop-sacks which the carter and his boy lift up to the drier. From the floor two short ladders lead to the doors in the cones where the hops are suspended on canvas floors above the kilns. The inside of the cone is full of coiling fumes which have killed the young swallows in the nests under the cowl—the parents return again and again, but dare no longer alight on their old perches on the vanes. When dried the hops are poured out on the floor of the vast chamber in a lisping scaly pile, and the drier is continually sweeping back those which are scattered. Through a hole in the floor he forces them down into a sack reaching to the floor of the room below. He is hard at work making these sacks or "pokes," which, when full and their necks stitched up, are as hard as wood. Before the drying is over the full sacks will take up half the room. The children tired of

picking come to admire and to visit all the corners of
the room; of the granary alongside and its old sheep-
bells, its traps, a crossbow and the like; of the farmyard
and barns, sacred except at this time. For a few minutes
the sun is visible as a shapeless crimson thing above the
mist and behind the elms. It is twilight; the wheels and
hoofs of the last waggon approach and arrive and die
away. And so day after day the fires glow with ruby
and sapphire and emerald; the cone wears its plume of
smoke; and everything is yellow-green—the very scent
of the drying hops can hardly be otherwise described,
in its mixture of sharpness and mellowness. Then
when the last sack is pressed benches are placed round
the chamber and a table at one end. The master, who
is giving up the farm, leans on the table and pays each
picker and pole-puller and measurer, with a special
word for each and a jest for the women. Ale and gin
and cakes are brought in, and the farmer leaves the
women and one or two older men to eat and drink.
The women in their shabby black skirts and whitish
blouses shuffle through a dance or two, all modern and
some American. One old man tipsily tottering recalls
the olden time with a step-dance down the room; some
laugh at him, others turn up their now roseate noses.
Next year the hops are to be grubbed up; the old man
to be turned out of his cottage—for he has paid no rent
these seven years; but now it is cakes and ale, and the
farmer has hiccupped a lying promise that his successor
will go on growing hops.

From " The South Country "

Here the spirit quickens and rejoices in perceptions of vitality, growth, the haunting presence of the past, agriculture, and the loveliness of some of the work of human skill and design. The eloquence is a means to convey excitement and extraordinary alertness. The phrasing, with touches of odd dignity, seems slightly old-fashioned; like Thomas's ways of feeling it owes much to the country prose of the great Richard Jefferies (about whom Thomas wrote one of his best books—a minor classic). That was some of the most durable, fresh, and vigorous prose of Victorian England. This has at the same time a relish of its own, a more indulgent fulness of feeling.

Thomas's prose work is uneven: there was too much of it, often composed to order and too fast. But the best carries a memorable and personal stamp, and the prose of his last years is very fine indeed. The books are hard to come by nowadays. There is a valuable selection, "The Prose of Edward Thomas" (Falcon Press). His "Collected Poems" (Faber and Faber) are available, and—for those who care to know more of Thomas as a man and a writer —so are "As it Was" and "World without End" (Heinemann). These short biographical narratives by his wife, Helen Thomas, are beautifully and movingly written.

Flowery Tuscany

D. H. Lawrence

We return to D. H. Lawrence for this final reading; to the writer whose descriptive power (if that is the term to apply) far exceeds any other's in our age. He has the sensuous perception, the intimate knowledge—he is an inspired botanist in the piece that follows. But he has also some apprehension of the inner sources of life—of what Wordsworth called 'unknown modes of Being'—in the growth, and colour, and splendour of the natural world about him. For Lawrence the scientific attitude, even when infused with the amazed respect of a Sherrington, could not sufficiently penetrate the reality behind nature. "The sun, I tell you, is alive, and more alive than I am or a tree is. It may have blazing gas as I have hair or a tree leaves. But I tell you it is the Holy Ghost in full raiment, shaking and walking, alive as a tiger, only more so."

The best way to prepare for 'Flowery Tuscany' is through the tribute of one of his friends, Aldous Huxley. In his diary, in 1927, he noted: "Of most other eminent people I have met I feel that at any rate I belong to the same species as they do. But this man has something different and superior in kind, not degree." And he adds (in his Introduction to "The Letters of D. H. Lawrence"), " I think almost everyone who knew him well must have felt that Lawrence was this. A being, somehow, of another order, more sensitive, more highly conscious, more capable of feeling than even the most gifted of common men. . . . To be with Lawrence was a kind of adventure, a voyage of discovery into newness and otherness. For, being himself of a different order, he inhabited a different universe from that of common men —a brighter and intenser world, of which while he spoke he would make you free. He looked at things with the eyes, so it seemed, of a man who had been at the brink of death and to whom, as he emerges from darkness, the world reveals itself as unfathomably beautiful and mysterious. . . . A walk with him in the country was a walk through that marvellously rich and significant landscape which is at once the background and the principal personage of all his novels. He seemed to know, by personal experience, what it was like to be a tree or a daisy or a breaking wave or even the mysterious moon itself."

NORTH of the Alps, the everlasting winter is interrupted by summers that struggle and soon yield; south of the Alps, the everlasting summer is interrupted by spasmodic and spiteful winters that never get a real hold, but that are mean and dogged. North of the Alps, you may have a pure winter's day in June. South of the Alps, you may have a midsummer day in December or January or even February. The inbetween, in either case, is just as it may be. But the lands of the sun are south of the Alps, for ever.

Yet things, the flowers especially, that belong to both sides of the Alps, are not much earlier south than north of the mountains. Through all the winter there are roses in the garden, lovely creamy roses, more pure and mysterious than those of summer, leaning perfect from the stem. And the narcissus in the garden are out by the end of January, and the little simple hyacinths early in February.

But out in the fields, the flowers are hardly any sooner than English flowers. It is mid-February before the first violets, the first crocus, the first primrose. And in mid-February one may find a violet, a primrose, a crocus in England, in the hedgerows and the garden corner.

And still there is a difference. There are several kinds of wild crocus in this region of Tuscany: being little spiky mauve ones, and spiky little creamy ones, that grow among the pine trees of the bare slopes. But the beautiful ones are those of a meadow in the corner of the woods, the low hollow meadow below the steep, shadowy pine-slopes, the secretive grassy dip where the water seeps through the turf all winter, where the stream runs between thick bushes, where the nightingale sings his mightiest in May, and where the wild thyme is rosy and full of bees, in summer.

Here the lavender crocuses are most at home—here sticking out of the deep grass, in a hollow like a cup, a bowl of grass, come the lilac-coloured crocuses, like an innumerable encampment. You may see them at twilight, with all the buds shut, in the mysterious stillness of the grassy underworld, palely glimmering like myriad folded tents. So the Apaches still camp, and close their tepees, in the hollows of the great hills of the West, at night.

But in the morning it is quite different. Then the sun shines strong on the horizontal green cloud-puffs of the pines, the sky is clear and full of life, the water runs hastily, still browned by the last juice of crushed olives.

And there the earth's bowl of crocuses is amazing. You cannot believe that the flowers are really still. They are open with such delight, and their pistil-thrust is so red-orange, and they are so many, all reaching out wide and marvellous, that it suggests a perfect ecstasy of radiant, thronging movement, lit-up violet and orange, and surging in some invisible rhythm of concerted, delightful movement. You cannot believe they do not move, and make some sort of crystalline sound of delight. If you sit still and watch, you begin to move with them, like moving with the stars, and you feel the sound of their radiance. All the little cells of the flowers must be leaping with flowery life and utterance.

And the small brown honey-bees hop from flower to flower, dive down, try, and off again. The flowers have been already rifled, most of them. Only sometimes a bee stands on his head, kicking slowly inside the flower, for some time. He has found something. And all the bees have little loaves of pollen, bee-bread, in their elbow-joints.

The crocuses last in their beauty for a week or so, and as they begin to lower their tents and abandon camp, the violets begin to thicken. It is already March. The violets have been showing like tiny dark hounds for some weeks. But now the whole pack comes forth, among the grass and the tangle of wild thyme, till the air all sways subtly scented with violets, and the banks above where the crocuses had their tents are now swarming brilliant purple with violets. They are the sweet violets of early spring, but numbers have made them bold, for they flaunt and ruffle till the slopes are a bright blue-purple blaze of them, full in the sun, with an odd late crocus still standing wondering and erect amongst them.

And now that it is March, there is a rush of flowers. Down by the other stream, which turns sideways to the sun, and has tangles of brier and bramble, down where the hellebore has stood so wan and dignified all winter, there are now white tufts of primroses, suddenly come. Among the tangle and near the water-lip, tufts and bunches of primroses, in abundance. Yet they look more wan, more pallid, more flimsy than English primroses. They lack some of the full wonder of the northern flowers. One tends to overlook them, to turn to the great, solemn-faced purple violets that rear up from the bank, and above all, to the wonderful little towers of the grape-hyacinth.

I know no flower that is more fascinating, when it first appears, than the blue grape-hyacinth. And yet, because it lasts so long, and keeps on coming so repeatedly, for at least two months, one tends later on to ignore it, even to despise it a little. Yet that is very unjust.

The first grape-hyacinths are flowers of blue, thick and rich and meaningful, above the unrenewed grass. The upper buds are pure blue, shut tight; round balls of pure, perfect warm blue, blue, blue; while the lower bells are darkish blue-purple, with the spark of white at the mouth. As yet, none of the lower bells has withered, to leave the greenish, separate sparseness of fruiting that spoils the grape-hyacinth later on, and makes it seem naked and functional. All hyacinths are like that in the seeding.

But, at first, you have only a compact tower of night-blue clearing to dawn, and extremely beautiful. If we were tiny as fairies, and lived only a summer, how lovely these great trees of bells would be to us, towers of night and dawn-blue globes. They would rise above us thick and succulent, and the purple globes would push the blue ones up, with white sparks of ripples, and we should see a god in them.

As a matter of fact, someone once told me they were the flowers of the many-breasted Artemis; and it is true, the Cybele of Ephesus, with her clustered breasts, was like a grape-hyacinth at the bosom.

This is the time, in March, when the sloe is white and misty in the hedge-tangle by the stream, and on the slope of land the peach tree stands pink and alone. The almond blossom, silvery pink, is passing, but the peach, deep-toned, bluey, not at all ethereal, this reveals itself like flesh, and the trees are like isolated individuals, the peach and the apricot.

A man said this spring: "Oh, I *don't* care for peach blossom! It is such a vulgar pink!" One wonders what anybody means by a "vulgar" pink. I think pink flannelette is rather vulgar. But probably it's the flannelette's fault, not the pink. And peach blossom has a beautiful sensual pink, far from vulgar, most rare and private. And pink is so beautiful in a landscape, pink houses, pink almond, pink peach and purply apricot, pink asphodels.

It is so conspicuous and so individual, that pink among the coming green of spring, because the first flowers that emerge from winter seem always white or yellow or purple. Now the celandines are out, and along the edges of the *podere*, the big, sturdy, black-purple anemones, with black hearts.

They are curious, these great, dark-violet anemones. You may pass them on a grey day, or at evening or early morning, and never see them. But as you come along in the full sunshine, they seem to be baying at you with all their throats, baying deep purple into the air. It is because they are hot and wide open now, gulping the sun. Whereas when they are shut, they have a silkiness and a curved head, like the curve of an umbrella handle, and a peculiar outward colourlessness, that makes them quite invisible. They may be under your feet, and you will not see them.

Altogether anemones are odd flowers. On these last hills above the plain, we have only the big black-purple ones, in tufts here and there, not many. But two hills away, the young green corn is blue with the lilac-blue kind, still the broad-petalled sort with the darker heart. But these flowers are smaller than our dark-purple, and frailer, more silky. Ours are substantial, thickly vegetable flowers and not abundant. The others are lovely and silky-delicate, and the whole corn is blue with them. And they have a sweet, sweet scent, when they are warm.

Then on the priest's *podere* there are the scarlet, Adonis-blood anemones: only in one place, in one long fringe under a terrace, and there by a path below. These flowers above all you will never find unless you look for them in the sun. Their silver silk outside makes them quite invisible, when they are shut up.

Yet, if you are passing in the sun, a sudden scarlet faces on to the air, one of the loveliest scarlet apparitions in the world. The inner surface of the Adonis-blood anemone is as fine as velvet, and yet there is no suggestion of pile, not as much as on a velvet rose. And from this inner smoothness issues the red colour, perfectly pure and unknown of earth, no earthiness, and yet solid, not transparent. How a colour manages to be perfectly strong and impervious, yet of a purity that suggests condensed light, yet not luminous, at least, not transparent is a problem. The poppy in her radiance is translucent, and the tulip in her utter redness has a touch of opaque earth. But the Adonis-blood anemone is neither translucent nor opaque. It is just pure condensed red, of a velvetiness without velvet, and a scarlet without glow.

This red seems to me the perfect premonition of summer—like the red on the outside of apple blossom —and later, the red of the apple. It is the premonition in redness of summer and of autumn.

The red flowers are coming now. The wild tulips are in bud, hanging their grey leaves like flags. They come up in myriads, wherever they get a chance. But they are holding back their redness till the last days of March, the early days of April.

Still, the year is warming up. By the high ditch the common magenta anemone is hanging its silky tassels, or opening its great magenta daisy-shape to the hot sun. It is much nearer to red than the big-petalled anemones are; except the Adonis-blood. They say these anemones spring from the tears of Venus, which fell as she went looking for Adonis. At that rate, how the poor lady must have wept, for the anemones by the Mediterranean are common as daisies in England.

The daisies are out here too, in sheets, and they too are red-mouthed. The first ones are big and handsome. But as March goes on, they dwindle to bright little things, like tiny buttons, clouds of them together. That means summer is nearly here.

The red tulips open in the corn like poppies, only with a heavier red. And they pass quickly, without repeating themselves. There is little lingering in a tulip.

In some places there are odd yellow tulips, slender, spiky and Chinese-looking. They are very lovely, pricking out their dulled yellow in slim spikes. But they too soon lean, expand beyond themselves, and are gone like an illusion.

And when the tulips are gone, there is a moment's pause, before summer. Summer is the next move.

In the pause towards the end of April, when the flowers seem to hesitate, the leaves make up their minds to come out. For some time, at the very ends of the bare boughs of fig trees, spurts of pure green have been burning like little cloven tongues of green fire vivid on the tips of the candelabrum. Now these spurts of green spread out, and begin to take the shape of hands, feeling for the air of summer. And tiny green figs are below them, like glands on the throat of a goat.

For some time, the long stiff whips of the vine have had knobby pink buds, like flower buds. Now these pink buds begin to unfold into greenish, half-shut fans of leaves with red in the veins, and tiny spikes of flower, like seed-pearls. Then, in all its down and pinky dawn, the vine-rosette has a frail, delicious scent of a new year.

Now the aspens on the hill are all remarkable with the translucent membranes of blood-veined leaves. They are gold-brown, but not like autumn, rather like the thin wings of bats when like birds—call them birds —they wheel in clouds against the setting sun, and the sun glows through the stretched membrane of their wings, as through thin, brown-red stained glass. This is the red sap of summer, not the red dust of autumn. And in the distance the aspens have the tender panting glow of living membrane just come awake. This is the beauty of the frailty of spring.

The cherry tree is something the same, but more sturdy. Now, in the last week of April, the cherry blossom is still white, but waning and passing away: it is late this year, and the leaves are clustering thick and softly copper in their dark blood-filled glow. It is queer about fruit trees in this district. The pear and the peach were out together. But now the pear tree is a lovely thick softness of new and glossy green, vivid with a tender fullness of apple-green leaves, gleaming among all the other green of the landscape, the half-high wheat, emerald, and the grey olive, half-invisible, the browning green of the dark cypress, the black of the evergreen oak, the rolling, heavy green puffs of the stone-pines, the flimsy green of small peach and almond trees, the sturdy young green of horse-chest-nut. So many greens, all in flakes and shelves and tilted tables and round shoulders and plumes and shaggles and uprisen bushes, of greens and greens, sometimes blindingly brilliant at evening, when the landscape looks as if it were on fire from inside, with greenness and with gold.

The pear is perhaps the greenest thing in the landscape. The wheat may shine lit-up yellow, or glow
bluish, but the pear tree is green in itself. The cherry
has white, half-absorbed flowers, so has the apple. But
the plum is rough with her new foliage, and inconspicuous, inconspicuous as the almond, the peach, the
apricot, which one can no longer find in the landscape,
though twenty days ago they were the distinguished
pink individuals of the whole countryside. Now they
are gone. It is the time of green, pre-eminent green, in
ruffles and flakes and slabs.

In the wood, the scrub-oak is only just coming un-
crumpled, and the pines keep their hold on winter.
They are wintry things, stone-pines. At Christmas,
their heavy green clouds are richly beautiful. When the
cypresses raise their tall and naked bodies of dark
green, and the osiers are vivid red-orange, on the still
blue air, and the land is lavender; then, in mid-winter,
the landscape is most beautiful in colour, surging with
colour.

But now, when the nightingale is still drawing out
his long, wistful, yearning, teasing plaint-note, and
following it up with a rich and joyful burble, the pines
and the cypresses seem hard and rusty, and the wood
has lost its subtlety and its mysteriousness. It still
seems wintry in spite of the yellowing young oaks, and
the heath in flower. But hard, dull pines above, and
hard, dull, tall heath below, all stiff and resistant, this
is out of the mood of spring.

In spite of the fact that the stone-white heath is in
full flower, and very lovely when you look at it, it does
not, casually, give the impression of blossom. More the

impression of having its tips and crests all dipped in hoarfrost; or in a whitish dust. It has a peculiar ghostly colourlessness amid the darkish colourlessness of the wood altogether, which completely takes away the sense of spring.

Yet the tall white heath is very lovely, in its invisibility. It grows sometimes as tall as a man, lifting up its spires and its shadowy-white fingers with a ghostly fullness, amid the dark, rusty green of its lower bushiness; and it gives off a sweet honeyed scent in the sun, and a cloud of fine white stone-dust, if you touch it. Looked at closely, its little bells are most beautiful, delicate and white, with the brown-purple inner eye and the dainty pin-head of the pistil. And out in the sun at the edge of the wood, where the heath grows tall and thrusts up its spires of dim white next a brilliant, yellow-flowering vetch-bush, under a blue sky, the effect has a real magic.

And yet, in spite of all, the dim whiteness of all the flowering heath-fingers only adds to the hoariness and out-of-date quality of the pine-woods, now in the pause between spring and summer. It is the ghost of the interval.

Not that this week is flowerless. But the flowers are little lonely things, here and there: the early purple orchid, ruddy and very much alive, you come across occasionally, then the little groups of bee-orchid, with their ragged concerted indifference to their appearance. Also there are the huge bud-spikes of the stout, thick-flowering pink orchid, huge buds like fat ears of wheat, hard-purple and splendid. But already odd grains of the wheat-ear are open, and out of the purple hangs the

delicate pink rag of a floweret. Also there are very
lovely and choice cream-coloured orchids with brown
spots on the long and delicate lip. These grow in the
more moist places, and have exotic tender spikes, very
rare-seeming. Another orchid is a little, pretty yellow
one.

But orchids, somehow, do not make a summer. They
are too aloof and individual. The little slate-blue
scabious is out, but not enough to raise an appearance.
Later on, under the real hot sun, he will bob into
notice. And by the edges of the paths there are odd rose
cushions of wild thyme. Yet these, too, are rather
samples than the genuine thing. Wait another month,
for wild thyme.

The same with the irises. Here and there, in fringes
along the upper edge of terraces, and in odd bunches
among the stones, the dark-purple iris sticks up. It is
beautiful, but it hardly counts. There is not enough of
it, and it is torn and buffeted by too many winds. First
the wind blows with all its might from the Mediterranean, not cold, but infinitely wearying, with its rude
and insistent pushing. Then, after a moment of calm,
back comes a hard wind from the Adriatic, cold and
disheartening. Between the two of them, the dark-
purple iris flutters and tatters and curls as if it were
burnt: while the yellow rock-rose streams at the end of
its thin stalk, and wishes it had not been in such a
hurry to come out.

There is really no hurry. By May, the great winds
will drop, and the great sun will shake off his harass-
ments. Then the nightingale will sing an unbroken song,
and the discreet, barely audible Tuscan cuckoo will be

a little more audible. Then the lovely pale-lilac irises will come out in all their showering abundance of tender, proud, spiky bloom, till the air will gleam with mauve, and a new crystalline lightness will be everywhere.

The iris is half-wild, half-cultivated. The peasants sometimes dig up the roots, iris root, orris root (orris powder, the perfume that is still used). So, in May, you will find ledges and terraces, fields just lit up with the mauve light of irises, and so much scent in the air, you do not notice it, you do not even know it. It is all the flowers of iris, before the olive invisibly blooms.

There will be tufts of iris everywhere, rising up proud and tender. When the rose-coloured wild gladiolus is mingled in the corn, and the love-in-the-mist opens blue: in May and June, before the corn is cut.

But as yet it is neither May nor June, but the end of April, the pause between spring and summer, the nightingale singing interruptedly, the bean-flowers dying in the bean-fields, the bean-perfume passing with spring, the little birds hatching in the nests, the olives pruned, and the vines, the last bit of late ploughing finished, and not much work to hand, now, not until the peas are ready to pick, in another two weeks or so. Then all the peasants will be crouching between the pea-rows, endlessly, endlessly gathering peas, in the long pea-harvest which lasts two months.

So the change, the endless and rapid change. In the sunny countries, the change seems more vivid, and more complete than in the grey countries. In the grey countries, there is a grey or dark permanency, over whose surface passes change ephemeral, leaving no real mark. In England, winters and summers shadowily give place to one another. But underneath lies the grey sub-stratum, the permanency of cold, dark reality where bulbs live, and reality is bulbous, a thing of endurance and stored-up, starchy energy.

But in the sunny countries, change is the reality and permanence is artificial and a condition of imprisonment. In the North, man tends instinctively to imagine, to conceive that the sun is lighted like a candle, in an everlasting darkness, and that one day the candle will go out, the sun will be exhausted, and the everlasting dark will resume uninterrupted sway. Hence, to the northerner, the phenomenal world is essentially tragical, because it is temporal and must cease to exist. Its very existence implies ceasing to exist, and this is the root of the feeling of tragedy.

But to the southerner, the sun is so dominant that, if every phenomenal body disappeared out of the universe, nothing would remain but bright luminousness, sunniness. The absolute is sunniness; and shadow, or dark, is only merely relative: merely the result of something getting between one and the sun.

This is the instinctive feeling of the ordinary southerner. Of course, if you start to *reason*, you may argue that the sun is a phenomenal body. Therefore it came into existence, therefore it will pass out of existence, therefore the very sun is tragic in its nature.

But this is just argument. We think, because we have to light a candle in the dark, therefore some First Cause had to kindle the sun in the infinite darkness of the beginning.

The argument is entirely shortsighted and specious.

We do not know in the least whether the sun ever came into existence, and we have not the slightest possible ground for conjecturing that the sun will ever pass out of existence. All that we do know, by actual experience, is that shadow comes into being when some material object intervenes between us and the sun, and that shadow ceases to exist when the intervening object is removed. So that, of all temporal or transitory or bound-to-cease things that haunt our existence, shadow, or darkness, is the one which is purely and simply temporal. We can think of death, if we like, as of something permanently intervening between us and the sun: and this is at the root of the southern, underworld idea of death. But this doesn't alter the sun at all. As far as experience goes, in the human race, the one thing that is always there is the shining sun, and dark shadow is an accident of intervention.

Hence, strictly, there is no tragedy. The universe contains no tragedy, and man is only tragical because he is afraid of death. For my part, if the sun always shines, and always will shine, in spite of millions of clouds of words, then death, somehow, does not have many terrors. In the sunshine, even death is sunny. And there is no end to the sunshine.

That is why the rapid change of the Tuscan spring is utterly free, for me, of any sense of tragedy. "Where are the snows of yesteryear?" Why, precisely where they ought to be. Where are the little yellow aconites of eight weeks ago? I neither know nor care. They were sunny and the sun shines, and sunniness means change, and petals passing and coming. The winter aconites sunnily came, and sunnily went. What more?

The sun always shines. It is our fault if we don't think so.

From " Phoenix "

" He sees more than a human being ought to see." " To be with him was to find oneself transported to one of the frontiers of human consciousness." So his friends spoke of him, and we can see why. This unforced utterance of the reality of growth and life, this unforced reverence before it, is unique. We may come near to it in some of his later verse, notably " Birds, Beasts and Flowers." It is valuable to turn to such verse as 'Bavarian Gentians' after 'Flowery Tuscany.' To enlarge one's understanding of these aspects of Lawrence's genius, there are four travel books; two of them, " Sea and Sardinia" and " Etruscan Places," have been published as Penguin books. 'Flowery Tuscany' itself appears in the Penguin " Selected Essays." Then there are the " Letters," (or a selection of them in Penguin books). Finally, his life and character are best seen through the eyes of three who knew him well: the Miriam of " Sons and Lovers" (" D. H. Lawrence: a Memoir," by E. T.), Catharine Carswell (" The Savage Pilgrimage"), and his wife, Frieda (" Not I, but the Wind").

Book List

Here is a list of the books from which these readings were taken:

D. H. LAWRENCE	*Phoenix* (Heinemann)
EDWIN MUIR	*An Autobiography* (Hogarth Press)
EDMUND BLUNDEN	*Undertones of War* (Bodley Head)
SIEGFRIED SASSOON	*The Complete Memoirs of George Sherston* (Faber and Faber)
ROBERT GRAVES	*Good-bye to All That* (Cape)
BEATRICE WEBB	*My Apprenticeship* (Longmans)
E. M. FORSTER	*Goldsworthy Lowes Dickinson* (Arnold)
ERIC GILL	*Autobiography* (Cape)
GEORGE STURT	*The Wheelwright's Shop* (Cambridge)
JOSEPH CONRAD	*The Mirror of the Sea* (Dent)
VIRGINIA WOOLF	*The Common Reader* (Hogarth Press)
CHARLES SHERRINGTON	*Man on his Nature* (Cambridge)
WILLIAM BRAGG	*Concerning the Nature of Things* (Bell)
EDWARD THOMAS	*The South Country* (Dent)

Here is a list of some of the books particularly referred to during the discussion of the readings, and probably available:

D. H. LAWRENCE	*Sons and Lovers* (Heinemann)
	The Rainbow (Heinemann)
	Birds, Beasts, and Flowers (Heinemann)
	Letters (Heinemann)

EDWIN MUIR	*Collected Poems* (Faber and Faber)
HERBERT READ	*Annals of Innocence and Experience* (Faber and Faber)
SIEGFRIED SASSOON	*Poems, newly selected* (Faber and Faber)
ROBERT GRAVES	*I, Claudius* (Penguin)
	Selected Poems (Penguin)
BEATRICE WEBB	*Our Partnership* (Longmans)
RONALD STORRS	*Orientations* (Nicholson)
G. E. MOORE	*Ethics* (H.U.L.)
E. M. FORSTER	*Where Angels fear to tread* (Arnold)
	A Passage to India (Penguin)
ERIC GILL	*In a Strange Land* (Cape)
GEORGE STURT	*The Bettesworth Book* (Duckworth)
	Change in the Village (Duckworth)
WILLIAM COBBETT	*Rural Rides* (Everyman)
RICHARD JEFFERIES	*Hodge and his Masters* (Faber and Faber)
ADRIAN BELL	*Corduroy* (Bodley Head)
JOSEPH CONRAD	*Typhoon, Shadow Line* (Everyman)
	Heart of Darkness (Dent)
	The Secret Agent (Dent)
VIRGINIA WOOLF	*To the Lighthouse* (Everyman)
WILLIAM BRAGG	*The World of Sound* (Bell)
	Old Trades and New Knowledge (Bell)
EDWARD THOMAS	*The Last Sheaf* (Cape)
	Childhood of Edward Thomas (Faber and Faber)
	Collected Poems (Faber and Faber)
ROLAND GANT	*The Prose of Edward Thomas* (Falcon Press)
HELEN THOMAS	*As it Was* and *World without End* (Heinemann)

Here is a list of those among all the foregoing which have been published as *Penguin* or *Pelican* books. Inclusion in this list does not necessarily mean that the book is currently available.

From the first list:

D. H. LAWRENCE	*Selected Essays*
EDMUND BLUNDEN	*Undertones of War*
BEATRICE WEBB	*My Apprenticeship*
VIRGINIA WOOLF	*The Common Reader*
CHARLES SHERRINGTON	*Man on his Nature*

From the second list:

D. H. LAWRENCE	*Sons and Lovers*
	The Rainbow
	Selected Letters
	Selected Poems
SIEGFRIED SASSOON	*Sherston's Progress*
ROBERT GRAVES	*I, Claudius*
	Selected Poems
E. M. FORSTER	*A Passage to India*
ADRIAN BELL	*Corduroy*